Triumph 650cc and 750cc Twins

Bonneville, Tiger, Trophy and Thunderbird

Matthew Vale

THE CROWOOD PRESS

First published in 2009 by
The Crowood Press Ltd
Ramsbury, Marlborough
Wiltshire SN8 2HR

www.crowood.com

British Library Cataloguing-in-Publication Data
A catalogue record for this book is available from the British Library.

ISBN 978 1 84797 120 3

Typeset and designed by D & N Publishing
Lambourn Woodlands, Hungerford, Berkshire

Printed and bound by Craft Print, Singapore

Contents

Acknowledgements

This is my fourth book, and I would like to thank all those involved in its preparation. These include my wife Julia and daughter Lizzie, who have put up with me disappearing into the study to write the book and sort out the pictures. Many thanks are due to Rowena Hoseason and Frank Westworth of RealClassic (*see* www.realclassic.co.uk) for a number of the pictures used. Finally I would like to thank my brother, Nick Vale, Peter Isted and Darren Babkirk for their anecdotes and the pictures of their bikes.

Introduction

As the 1960s started, the Triumph Engineering Company Ltd was riding the crest of a wave. Its model range covered all the bases, comprising the 200cc single-cylinder Tiger Cub for the learner and commuter, the 350cc and 500cc 'C' range twins for the mid-range buyers and the big pre-unit 650cc bikes for the committed enthusiast. With this good market coverage and buoyant sales, especially in the US market, Triumph looked to update the oldest part of its range, the big pre-unit twins. These could trace their ancestry directly back to the 1938 500cc Speed Twin, with their separate engines and gearbox, and were in need of modernization.

This book looks at the range of unit construction 'B' Series 650cc and 750cc twins first introduced in 1963 for the 1964 model year. The 650cc models were the range leaders for Triumph through the 1960s until the 750cc Trident was introduced in 1968 and, with the 750cc version of the twin, were the last volume production British bikes produced through

The 1969 T120 is right at the pinnacle of the development of the first generation of the Triumph 'B' series twins. With good handling and roadholding, excellent performance and reliability, the bikes were probably the best 650 twins the British industry produced.

ABOVE: *The 1977 T140 in US specification is probably the best looking of the 750cc twins. Slim lines, light weight and reasonable performance add up to a package that is hard to beat.*

LEFT: *The last of the original Triumph twins was the Harris or 'Devon' Bonneville, built by Les Harris in Newton Abbot, South Devon. It used Italian suspension and wheel rims.*

While many books have charted the history and development of the 'top of the range' T120 Bonneville, the unit 650 range featured a well-balanced selection of touring and on/off-road sports bikes. These bikes were each aimed at a particular market and all sold well alongside the Bonneville, Triumph's ultimate twin-cylinder, twin-carburettor sports bike. In fact, these 'lesser' models probably offered the average rider a better compromise for 'normal' riding, being in a softer state of tune that made them more tractable and less highly strung than the Bonneville. However, it has to be conceded that it is the Bonneville that everyone recognizes and was (and still is) acknowledged as the 'top dog' machine of all the British bikes made during the mid-1960s.

the 1970s and into the early 1980s. The last 750cc models were the bikes that kept the Triumph name alive in the shape of the 'Devon' Triumphs from 1984 until John Bloor reintroduced the Triumph name to the mass production bike market in the 1990s.

1 Triumph 'B' Series Twins

A Brief History of Triumph

Triumph as a company started in 1885, set up by Siegfried Bettmann initially as an import-export company with interests in reselling pedal cycles and sewing machines. In 1887 Bettmann formed a partnership with Mauritz Johann Schulte, and the Triumph Cycle Co started to manufacture its own pedal cycles in Coventry. The company started to manufacture its own motorcycles in 1902. Triumph supplied some 30,000 motorbikes to the allied forces during the First World War, and their performance and reliability gained them the nickname of the 'Trusty Triumph'. After the war Triumph continued to expand and in 1923 started to produce cars as well as bikes. However, the 1930s depression put paid to many established companies and by the mid-1930s the company was in trouble. Jack Sangster, then owner of Ariel, heard about Triumph's problems and bought the motorcycle part of the business and formed the Triumph Engineering Co Ltd in 1936. As part of this takeover, Sangster appointed Edward Turner, a talented young designer who worked for Sangster at Ariel, as Chief Designer and General Manager. Sangster gave Edward Turner a relatively free hand, and this resulted in the

Edward Turner's 1930s Tiger 90 set the Triumph style that would endure for almost fifty years.
The 'Triumph look' was still present in the Harris Bonnevilles that were made until the late 1980s.

autocratic Turner running Triumph almost as his personal fiefdom.

Edward Turner's first task on taking over was to revamp Triumph's range of somewhat lacklustre singles, which he achieved swiftly and competently, more than repaying Sangster's faith in him. Edward Turner restyled the 250cc, 350cc and 500cc singles in the existing range and gave the models new, snappy and memorable names – the Tiger 70, 80 and 90 – to reflect their notional top speeds.

The 'new' bikes were very well styled and popular, and gave a new lease of life to the re-energized Triumph Company. Having got the company back on its feet, Edward Turner than pulled off his masterstroke that moulded the future of Triumph, and arguably the whole British industry, by designing and getting into production the evocatively named 500cc twin-cylinder Speed Twin. The new engine was designed to fit into the existing 500cc singles' frame and caused a sensation when it was introduced to the market in July 1937.

The success of the Speed Twin was helped by its slim engine: from a distance it could be mistaken for a twin port single, so did not alienate those riders who liked the look of a single. In typical Turner fashion, Turner then introduced a sports version of the 500cc twin, the Tiger 100, in 1939.

At the start of the Second World War Triumph's Coventry works turned to producing

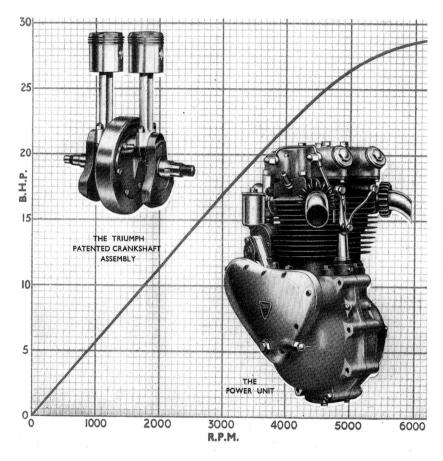

THE TRIUMPH
PATENTED CRANKSHAFT
ASSEMBLY

THE
POWER UNIT

The pre-unit Triumph twin engine lent its layout, head design and many details to the 650 unit engine. The looks of the pre-unit engine were faithfully reproduced in the unit-construction motor.

machines for the War Department in the shape of the 3SW and 5SW, 350cc and 500cc side-valve singles. However, Edward Turner designed a 350cc twin, the 3TW, that was based on the civilian 3T engine but with a three-speed gear-box in unit with the engine. It was light and agile and in late 1940 the War Department passed it for production. Unfortunately, fate intervened as the first pre-production batch of fifty machines was being prepared, and on the night of 14 November 1940 the Luftwaffe blitzed Coventry and the Triumph factory was destroyed. Triumph was relocated to a tempo-rary factory in Warwick, while a new purpose-built factory was built and fitted out at Meriden. This facility opened in May 1942 and production resumed. It was not the 3TW 350cc twin that Meriden produced, however,

but rather a 350cc single, the 3HW, based on the pre-war overhead valve single-cylinder model. Meriden also produced twin-cylinder engines based on the Speed Twin unit in the form of lightweight portable electric genera-tors for the Army and the Royal Air Force.

At the end of the war Triumph found itself with the most modern, purpose-built motor-cycle factory in the UK, equipped with many modern machine tools, and started to produce the 500cc Speed Twin and Tiger 100, alongside the 350cc 3H single and a new 350cc 3T twin. Triumph's markets were mainly overseas in the immediate post-war years, with Britain desper-ate to export goods to repay the debts incurred during the war, and this early focus on exports, especially to the USA, formed the basis for Triumph's success.

The Speed Twin was the start of the Triumph-twin lineage.

The 6T Thunderbird was an important part of the Triumph range, but the quest for increased performance and sports specifications led to its demise in 1966.

The US market was expanding rapidly and Triumph pursued it with high-performance machines such as the Tiger 100 alongside the Speed Twin. There were never-ending demands from the USA for ever more performance. Based on the US adage that there was 'no substitute for cubes', the 500cc engine was bored and stroked to 650cc and the 6T Thunderbird was introduced to the range. This model was complemented by the sportier 650cc Tiger 110 in 1954, with a higher tuned engine giving the Americans even more performance. In the late 1950s Triumph introduced the unit 350cc Twenty-one, which then grew into the 500cc 5TA in 1958. This replaced the pre-unit 500cc models, and left the 650cc Thunderbird and Tiger 110 as the only pre-unit models in

the range. The iconic 650cc T120 Bonneville was introduced for the 1959 season, with production beginning in September 1958. However, time caught up with the venerable design, and for the 1963 season Triumph replaced the pre-unit models with all new 650cc unit models: the 6T Thunderbird, the TR6 Trophy and the T120 Bonneville.

During the 1950s Triumph was incredibly successful in the USA with its unbeatable combination of performance and styling. Even though rivals such as BSA had a wider range of bikes, Triumph became the pre-eminent British make in the USA and in turn became increasingly reliant on that market. Despite BSA being Triumph's main rival in the USA (and the UK), it was not generally publicized at the time that in March 1951 Sangster sold Triumph to the BSA group, mainly to avoid paying punitive death duties. As part of the deal, Sangster became a director of BSA and later became Chairman of BSA in 1956. Edward Turner was made Managing Director of the BSA automotive division, which covered BSA, Triumph, Ariel, Sunbeam and New Hudson, as well as Daimler cars. Sangster retired in 1960, handing over his chairmanship to Eric Turner (who was no relation to Edward Turner). Edward Turner remained in his post as Managing Director until he retired in 1964.

Despite the merger, BSA and Triumph operated largely independently for many years (and indeed competed vigorously in most markets) with only limited cooperation on the design of the models in the separate ranges. While some components (such as wheel hubs and brakes) were shared in the 1960s, and some 'badge engineering' was carried out, notably in the production of the TR25W Trophy model, closely based on the BSA B25 Starfire, the lack of cooperation between Meriden and Small Heath was exemplified by the Triumph Trident/BSA Rocket Three models.

The TR25W Trophy was the epitome of BSA/Triumph badge engineering. It was a thinly disguised B25 Starfire and was even built at BSA's Small Heath plant.

These bikes were effectively two different models with only the engine layout in common. Both were 750cc triples, but, rather than sharing major components, they had completely different frames and engine casings, thus losing many possible economies of scale in their production. The evidence of real cooperation and cost savings by using common components only arrived in the 1971 model year, with a total revamp of the BSA and Triumph ranges. However, rather than making necessary changes and replacing the outmoded engines across both the BSA and Triumph ranges, the management fixed the bits that were not broken by replacing the frames and running gear of both the BSA

The T150 Trident was another example of badge engineering with its BSA Rocket Three cousin. The Trident's engine layout, however, was based on the Triumph twin. The bikes did not sell well until the styling was changed to resemble the Bonneville!

and Triumph 650cc twin models and the unit singles range, and kept the existing engines. The revamp of the range was intended to stem the decreases in profits, which had fallen in 1969 and 1970, and cost a fortune. The new range was not successful, however, and BSA posted a massive loss of more than £8,000,000 in 1971. Things were little better in 1972 with losses of £3,300,000. In 1973 the BSA name was dropped and the group was taken over by Norton Villiers, owned by Dennis Poore of Manganese Bronze Holdings. The new group, Norton Villiers Triumph, or NVT, proposed to close the Triumph plant at Meriden as a cost-cutting exercise and relocate all production to the BSA Small Heath plant.

This led to the Meriden workers barricading themselves in the plant in September 1973, in what became known as the Meriden Sit-in. No Triumphs were produced from this time until the end of the blockade, but the workers did release some batches of completed machines during the sit-in. Eventually the workers were able to form a co-operative (the Co-op) in March 1975. Production of Triumphs was restarted, but the plant only produced the 'B-Series' twins, although a number of 1973-built 'C-Series' 500cc Twins were released when the blockade was lifted. The Co-op limped on in Meriden until 1983, when the venture finally collapsed. The Triumph name and factory were bought by property developer John Bloor, who licensed production of the 750cc twin to Les Harris, who resumed manufacture from a factory in Devon for a few years in the late 1980s. Eventually Bloor was to resurrect Triumph with a completely new and up-to-date model range built in a new factory in Hinckley, Leicestershire, in the 1990s.

The Vertical Twin in Context

It is generally accepted that the 360-degree vertical twin was the definitive British motorcycle of the post-war era. Edward Turner's 500cc

Triumph Speed Twin first hit the road in the late 1930s and the vertical twin Turner designed had a number of significant features that assured its success. Principally, the Triumph twin was almost as light and slim as, but more powerful and smoother than, the singles that preceded it. The layout provided the right bike at the right time, and all of the major British manufacturers rushed to get their own twins into production after the Second World War. AJS, Ariel, BSA, Norton, Royal Enfield and Matchless all produced their own take on the twin, all starting at 500cc. These first-generation twins, including Triumph's, were pre-unit, with a separate engine and gearbox connected by a chain-drive sitting in a separate chain case containing the clutch that joined the engine and gearbox together – lots of joints and hence oil leaks. As time went on these twins were to grow and contract to provide various capacities from 350cc through 600cc, 650cc, 700cc, 750cc and finally, with the Norton Commando, 828cc. It was generally accepted that the optimal engine size was 650cc, which gave an acceptable balance of performance, vibration and reliability. Larger capacities just had too much metal thrashing around, and most 750cc twins were usually in a softer state of tune than a fast 650cc. Norton, of course, got round the vibration problem with its rubber mounting system (dubbed Isolastic, from 'isolate' and 'elastic', the two terms describing the characteristics of the system) on the Commando, and Royal Enfield gave a great deal of attention to dynamically balancing their 700cc Constellation and 736cc Interceptor, but both these solutions just masked the symptom rather than fixing the problem.

Only BSA and Triumph produced a second generation of their vertical twin engines, with the engine crankcases, chain cases and gearboxes all combined into a single set of two castings. The advantages of this system were many with fewer parts (hence lighter and cheaper), fewer joints (hence less chance of oil leaks) and simpler maintenance.

The Triumph 650cc unit motor resembled the pre-unit version with clearly defined engine and gearbox.

The unit construction twin engine configuration first appeared in a commercially successful Triumph at the end of the 1950s with the Triumph 21 350cc model, and the configuration was adopted by both BSA and Triumph for their larger twins in the early 1960s. The Triumph 350cc, 500cc 'C' Series twins and the 650cc and 750cc 'B' Series twins formed the mainstay of the Triumph range from the glory days of the British motorcycle industry in the early 1960s through its decline in the early 1970s, when the 750cc unit was left to soldier on alone until its final demise in 1988.

Why Unit Construction?

As the Swinging Sixties emerged from the austere 1950s, the engines of two out of the three bikes in the Triumph model range – the 200cc

The drive side of the Triumph unit had a styling flash cast into the primary drive cover. The whole unit was shorter than the pre-unit assembly.

Tiger Cub single-cylinder and the 350cc and 500cc 'C' Series twins – were 'unit construction' (that is, the engine, primary drive and gearbox were encased in a single pair of light alloy castings). This gave a large number of advantages over the previous generation of 'pre-unit' construction models as used in the 650cc models in the early 1960s. Unit construction gave precise alignment of the engine, gearbox and primary drive, was lighter, more rigid and more compact than the older style of construction. Fewer parts were required and the whole unit was easier to build and fit in the frame – giving rise to significant cost savings in both the parts that made up the unit itself and labour when constructing the bikes on the production line. So the updating of the 650cc range to

unit construction was inevitable, spurred on by a number of other factors. Lucas, Triumph's main supplier of electrical components, was planning to drop manufacture of magnetos and all the manufacturers were keen to change to the much cheaper coil ignition system Lucas was offering. These systems were not only significantly cheaper than a magneto, but were also lighter and much easier to integrate into an engine's design: a four-stroke needed just two contact breakers to be fixed on the end of a camshaft to give a simple and reliable ignition system. There was no need for the costly precision drives required by a magneto. Lucas had also recently introduced an alternator that could be driven directly off the crankshaft and could be placed in the primary chain case of most British twins to provide a reliable and cheap source of electricity to drive the new coil ignition system, which rendered the separate dynamo obsolete.

In addition, BSA, which had owned Triumph since 1951, was replacing its pre-unit 500cc A7 and 650cc A10 range with the unit construction A50 and A65 range, which was probably the Triumph big twins' main competitor at the time. So the move to unit construction for Triumph 650s was inevitable – but probably the most significant factor was that Triumph could build a better, more modern product that would sell for more money but cost significantly less to produce: as ever, economics wins!

It also made for a more compact design, and enabled the power unit to be styled as a whole, although Triumph went out of its way to retain a 'pre-unit' look, in stark contrast to BSA's A65 'water melon' motor. Press comments at the time and opinion today generally agree that the Triumph unit is better looking than the rather bland BSA engine, despite its deliberate nod to the past with the unit's styling aping the pre-unit look, with its deliberate separation of the engine and gearbox. Neither factory, however, went the whole way with the concept: both had separate chambers for the gearbox, crankshaft and primary drive rather than sharing the space and the oil between the three parts as the Italians and Japanese tended to do.

The Triumph unit 650cc and 750cc range mirrored the fall of the British motorcycle industry, in that it was another refinement of a basic design that was revolutionary in the 1930s but was virtually outdated when the first unit twin hit the road. It seemed that the creative spirit from the 1920s to the 1950s, which had taken the British motorcycle industry to its peak of engineering excellence, had died and the best that it could do was refine and develop what had gone before, rather than set a new trend.

'B' Series Twins

Introduced in 1963, the new 650cc range comprised three models: the touring 6T Thunderbird, the sporting TR6 Trophy and the out-and-out sports T120 Bonneville. Over the years the range was refined and developed, and the Bonneville especially became the epitome of the sports bike in the mid-1960s in both the UK and the USA. The more sophisticated Japanese opposition, however, was beginning to show the way forward for motorcycles in terms of refinement, engineering sophistication, reliability and comfort.

The Triumph twins' increasing levels of tune were beginning to show the inherent faults in the design. Vibration levels were becoming an issue by the mid-1960s. The higher states of tune also increased the potential for oil leaks as the engines became more stressed and impacted on the motors' reliability. Triumph was aware of these problems and the position of the 650 twins as Triumph's top model was taken over by the 750cc three-cylinder Trident, which offered more performance and less vibration. However, the Trident lost one of the twin's major marketing assets — it just did not look as good. It was also heavier and lacked some of the twin's simplicity, while not being as sophisticated as the Japanese opposition. These factors resulted in the 650cc models continuing in production along-

side the Trident, and indeed led to the 650 being stretched to 750cc. The industrial turmoil that the British motorcycle industry suffered in the early 1970s resulted in the eventual demise of Norton Villiers Triumph, but the Meriden Co-op continued to produce the twins until 1983, when it too failed. The Triumph name and assets were bought by John Bloor, who granted a licence for the production of the 750cc twins to Les Harris, while Bloor started to design and develop a complete new range of Triumphs.

The TSS 8-valve was the ultimate development of the Triumph unit engine. Its bottom end was beefed up to take the extra power.

Production of the Bonneville resumed in 1985 at Les Harris's new factory at Newton Abbot, Devon. The last Devon-built Triumph twins eventually rolled off the production line in March 1988. This gave the Triumph twin engine a life of (almost) continuous production of some fifty years: from the original Turner-designed Speed Twin of 1938 to Les Harris's final Bonneville of 1988. By any measure this is an impressive record that will probably not be matched again.

LEFT: The terms of their licence meant that the Harris bikes had to mirror the specification of the last T140s and they were not allowed to take advantage of the modification made to the TSS. However, they are generally acknowledged to be fine engines with excellent component quality and careful assembly.

BELOW: Nick Vale's 1977 T140V and the author's 1970 T120R Bonnevilles make a striking contrast on Hartley Wintney's cricket green. The pair represent what are probably the best Bonnevilles made.

2 Model Development, 1963–70: The First Generation

The new Triumph 'B' Range, with its unit-construction engine and gearbox, was introduced for the 1963 model year and initially comprised three 650cc Unit Twins: the 6T Thunderbird, the TR6 Trophy and the T120 Bonneville. A fourth model, the TR6R Tiger, was introduced in 1969.

One minor but significant departure from the previous models was the introduction of ⅞in (21mm) diameter handlebars, rather than retaining the Triumph trademark 1in (25mm) diameter unit used on the pre-unit 650s. As the model evolved, several specialist variants emerged, notably the Police bikes, as epitomized by the Saint and special racing models, the road-racing Thruxton Bonneville and the off-road racing T120TT designed for dirt-track racing in the USA.

The history of the models is presented in two halves: this chapter addresses the models with separate oil tanks, produced between 1963 and 1970, while Chapter 3 addresses the oil-in-frame models produced at Meriden from 1970 to 1983 and by Les Harris in Newton Abbot from 1985 until production of the model finally ceased in 1988. The technical changes applied across the whole model range are described in Chapter 7.

The 6T Thunderbird was an important model in Triumph's line-up in 1963. Here the new unit-construction model is featured in a modernist setting on the front of Triumph's 1963 model year brochure.

17

The 1968 to 1970 models are generally considered to be the best of the bunch. The 1968 Trophy had the looks and performance – with its single carburettor it stayed in tune longer than the Bonneville.

Soft Tourer:
the Triumph Thunderbird

When the Thunderbird model was originally unveiled in 1949 for the 1950 model year, it was top of Triumph's sports machine range. Derived from the 500cc Speed Twin, the model 6T was launched in a blaze of publicity that culminated in three Thunderbirds covering 500 miles (805km) each at an average speed of more than 92mph (148km/h) at the French racing circuit of Montlhéry. Four Thunderbirds (one as a spare) were ridden to the track from Meriden by Triumph men Neil Shilton, Tyrell Smith, Alex Scobie and Len Bayliss. At the track they were joined by Allan Jefferies, Jim Alves and

Bob Manns. The aim of the test was achieved with all three machines averaging more than 90mph (145km/h) for the full 500 miles. The icing on the cake came when the three bikes went back out each to do a lap at more than 100mph (161km/h). This event placed the Thunderbird firmly at the top of Triumph's performance tree and was a spectacular launch for an impressive and successful model.

By the late 1950s, however, the Thunderbird was no longer the top-of-the-range 650 model. The single-carburettor Tiger 110 was faster and sportier on the road, the Trophy 650 was the off-road sportster and the twin-carburettor Bonneville was the undisputed king of the coffee bars. This left the Thunderbird at the

bottom of the 650cc range and, to quote the Triumph publicity of the time, it was sold to the public as a 'firm favourite with the hard riding solo or sidecar man'.

Following the introduction of the unit 650 twins in 1963, the Thunderbird remained in the range as a tourer, with its single-carburettor engine and extensive bodywork. However, with its keen price and a softly tuned motor

giving a healthy 34bhp, the Thunderbird found a ready market in the UK as a reliable and torquey all-round motorcycle with none of the temperament of the more highly tuned twins.

The Thunderbird carried on the tradition for enclosure started by the Triumph Twenty-one, the 350cc twin introduced in 1957. By 1963, however, Triumph had recognized that the full 'bathtub' enclosure, as used on the original Twenty-one and the pre-unit Thunderbird, was not very popular, so the unit Thunderbird had a smaller enclosure that covered the bike's 'middle' (the so-called 'bikini') and it was fitted with a conventional blade-type rear mudguard.

The bikini kept the area behind the engine clean and sleek, and was complemented by the traditional Triumph nacelle enclosing the steering head and headlamp and a large 'Roman helmet' style front mudguard. This was all very good for both protecting the rider from road dirt and making it easy to clean the machine, but was not appealing to the emerging youth market. The model was described at its introduction as: 'The machine is the choice of the discriminating rider who asks for the best in tractability, braking and suspension.'

ABOVE: The Thunderbird's front fork stanchions were protected from the elements with steel shrouds, while the other bikes in the range had sporty rubber bellows. The 1964 year external spring forks seen here meant the shrouds were slightly larger in diameter than the original nacelle.

Underneath the enclosure, the Thunderbird shared the single down-tube frame and bolt-on rear sub-frame with the rest of the 650s; only the 1963 model had rider's footrests mounted on the lower frame rails. The steel bikini and nacelle, Roman helmet front mudguard and 18in-diameter front wheel were unique to the Thunderbird, and the model would retain the nacelle in this incarnation until its deletion from the range in 1965. Brakes were the same as the rest of the 650cc range with an 8in (20.3cm) single leading shoe (SLS) front and 7in (17.7cm) SLS at the rear. The electrics remained at 6V, but AC power was supplied from the Lucas alternator in the primary chain case.

The bike was finished in a smart but understated black and silver colour scheme. The fuel tank top, nacelle and front-fork shrouds and frame were black, with the fuel tank lowers, bikini enclosure, fork sliders and mudguards in silver.

For 1964 the Thunderbird remained much the same, but there were a number of fairly major changes. In common with the rest of the

The Thunderbird's classic black and silver paintwork gave it a restrained and tasteful appearance. Here a 1966 model shows the 'Thunderbird' name on the side panel in Triumph's 'toothpaste' script.

THE ZENER-DIODE AS FITTED TO THE 12 VOLT THUNDERBIRD. THIS IS A VOLTAGE REGULATOR CONTROLLING THE RATE OF CHARGING TO THE BATTERIES.

LEFT: The Thunderbird pioneered the use of 12-volt electrics on the range. The zener diode, used to regulate the voltage, was mounted under the fuel tank on a large alloy heat sink.

RIGHT: Triumph still featured the Thunderbird on the cover of its 1964 brochure – a classic bit of 1960s nostalgia!

range the front forks were changed to external spring type, with new chromed seal carriers screwed to the top of the fork sliders. In contrast to the sporting rubber gaiters over the springs, the Thunderbird's forks retained their nacelle with fatter black steel shrouds over the springs. The footrest location was moved from the lower frame rail to the rear engine plates, increasing ground clearance. Finally, and uniquely to the Thunderbird, the electrics were uprated from 6V to 12V. Incorporated into the system was a zener diode, which enabled proper regulation of the charging circuit at last, and twin 6V batteries in series were fitted under the seat in a revised battery carrier. The zener diode was mounted on a large alloy plate heat sink, which was carefully fixed under the front of the fuel tank in the cooling breeze. Finally, a magnetic speedometer replaced the previous chronometric type.

The 1965 Thunderbird was given a slight power boost, up to 37bhp at 6,700rpm, and gained a slimmer, more sporting front mudguard. The troublesome oil pressure warning plunger on the oil pressure release valve was deleted, removing a source of oil leaks. Finish remained black and silver and the bike retained the bikini rear enclosure.

The final year for the original Thunderbird, in both the UK and US markets, was 1966. Still keeping its black and silver colour scheme, the

1966 Thunderbird was modified in line with the other models, with the lighter flywheel and pressure oil feed to the exhaust camshaft. The frame's steering head angle was reduced from 65 to 63 degrees and the eyebrow-style tank badge appeared. Power was now a claimed 40bhp. The bike at last lost its bikini enclosure, but retained the nacelle and steel fork shrouds. Strangely, the zener diode mount was moved behind the new left-hand side panel, where it was shielded from the cooling breeze. By

1966 the requirement for a softly tuned commuter/tourer had virtually disappeared. The sports market was dominant, especially in the USA, and Triumph could sell all the TR6s and T120s it could make. So the Thunderbird was dropped from the range at the end of the 1966 model year. This was not quite the end for the Thunderbird as the model was reintroduced into the range in 1981 with the 650cc oil-in-frame model, the TR65 (*see* Chapter 3).

First and Last Thunderbird 6T/TR65			
	1963 Thunderbird 6T	*1966 Thunderbird 6T*	*1983 Thunderbird TR65*
Engine			
Bore/stroke (mm)	71 × 82	71 × 82	76 × 71.5
Capacity (cc)	649	649	649
Compression ratio	7.5:1	7.5:1	8.6:1
Power (bhp @ rpm)	34 @ 6,300	40 @ 6,300	Not given
Carburettor			
Type	Amal Monobloc	Amal Monobloc	Amal Concentric Mk1
Specification	376/285	376/303	930/108
Number	1	1	1
Transmission			
Engine sprocket (teeth)	29	29	29
Clutch sprocket (teeth)	58	58	58
Gearbox sprocket (teeth)	20	20	19
Gearbox sprocket – sidecar (teeth)	–	18	–
Rear sprocket (teeth)	46	46	47
RPM, 10mph top gear	616	616	660
Gear ratios (sidecar)			
Fifth	–	–	4.95
Fourth	4.60:1	4.60 (5.11):1	5.89:1
Third	5.47:1	5.47 (6.08):1	6.93:1
Second	7.77:1	7.77 (8.64) :1	9.09:1
First	11.47:1	11.47 (11.81) :1	12.79:1
Wheels and tyres			
Front – size	3.25 × 18	3.25 × 18	3.25 × 19
Rear – size	3.50 × 18	3.50 × 18	4.00 × 18
Front Brake	8in SLS	8in SLS	9.8in disc
Rear Brake	7in SLS	7in SLS	7in SLS drum
Dimensions			
Seat height	30in (76.2cm)	30in (76.2cm)	31in (78.7cm)
Wheelbase	55in (139.6cm)	55in (139.6cm)	56in (142.2cm)
Length	84in (213.5cm)	84in (213.5cm)	87in (222cm)
Width	27½in (70cm)	27in (68.5cm)	32in (84cm)
Ground clearance	5in (12.7cm)	5in (12.7cm)	–
Weight	369lb (167kg)	369lb (167kg)	395lb (179.5kg)
Fuel capacity	4gal (18.2ltr)	4gal (18.2ltr)	4gal (18.2ltr)
Oil capacity	5 pints (2.8ltr)	6 pints (3.4ltr)	4 pints (2.27ltr)

Single-Carburettor Sportsters: TR6 Trophy and Tiger, 1963–70

Sitting between the softly tuned Thunderbird and the twin-carburettor super sports Bonneville was the TR6 range. The TR6 was, in essence, a single-carburettor sports bike. Over the years it carried various names and designations, but the range was essentially split between on- and off-road oriented models. When first introduced in 1963 the model was named Trophy, keeping the tradition set by the pre-unit off-road sports models. The Tiger name was resurrected in 1969 for the US market with the

The first unit construction TR6 Trophy was a classic looker. Note the footrests mounted on the lower frame members, which only featured on the 1963 models.

There are a lot of TR6s around today. This nice late 1960s model was seen at Shepton Mallet in Somerset in October 2008: note the 3½ gal US tank and US bars – an attractive combination.

The USA got all the best bikes! This export TR6C sports high-level exhausts, small headlamp and folding footrests, typical fitments denied to the UK market.

introduction of the TR6R Tiger, which was a renamed Trophy 'road sports' model, while the Trophy name remained for the 'off-road' TR6C model. In the UK the 'Tiger' name was not introduced until 1971, when it graced the new oil-in-frame single-carburettor 650cc road model, and was marketed alongside the high piped oil-in-frame Trophy for that year. The 'Trophy' name disappeared in the UK in 1972, leaving just the T120 Bonneville and TR6 Tiger in the 'B' series range. The Trophy name was eventually dropped in the USA in 1973 when the 'B' range models contracted to just the Tiger and Bonneville road models. The following paragraphs describe the main details of the TR6 models produced between 1963 and 1970. (For a description of the technical changes that were applied across the whole range of models, *see* Chapter 7.)

The first full year of production of the unit 650s (1963) saw the US export market being presented with the Trophy Road Sports (TR6S/R) with low pipes, and TR6S/C Trophy Competition, also with low-level pipes. Both models were finished with a flamboyant Regal Purple over Silver tank with silver-painted mudguards. For the UK there was just the TR6S/S Trophy, essentially a road-oriented model with low siamesed exhaust pipes with a single silencer on the right-hand side. The UK and general export bikes were finished like the US models in Regal Purple over Silver tank and silver guards. The Canadian market received a machine designated TR6SS (in effect a UK TR6S/S) and some of these were also imported into the USA.

For 1964 the single-carburettor models were similar to the previous year, with the model designations and names remaining the same: the USA saw the Trophy Road Sports (TR6S/R), with low exhaust pipes and large 'resonator' silencers, and the TR6S/C Trophy Competition, which was equipped more appropriately, in view of its off-road aspirations, with high-level pipes. The TR6S/C high-level pipes swept over the top of the crankcases on each side, were equipped with heat shields for the rider's leg, and had small straight-through-type silencers. The models gained the external spring front forks and the new footrests fitted to the engine plates to increase ground clearance. The TR6S/R and TR6S/C were both finished in Flamboyant Scarlet over Silver on the fuel tank with silver mudguards. For the UK market, again, there was just the TR6 Trophy, but it now sported twin low-level exhaust

pipes and silencers. The UK and general export models were finished in Hi-Fi Scarlet over Silver tank and silver guards.

In 1965 the USA saw the Trophy Road Sports (TR6S/R) model with low-level exhaust pipes, finished in Burnished Gold over Alaskan White, with white mudguards, and the TR6S/C came with high-level pipes (one each side) and alloy mudguards. For the UK there was just the TR6 Trophy, with low pipes and also finished with a Burnished Gold over Alaskan White fuel tank and white guards.

There were some significant changes to the export range in 1966 as Triumph started to address the specific requirements of its largest market. These included the signature slim small-capacity fuel tanks and high and wide western-style handlebars. This started off the look that

The 1968 TR6 Trophy had the looks and the equipment. The twin leading shoe
front brake was acknowledged as one of the best brakes the industry produced.

LEFT: *Sporting alloy rims and Dunlop TT100 tyres, this 1968 Trophy has the sensible modifications that enhance riding pleasure without compromising originality.*

OPPOSITE TOP: *This 1970 TR6 Trophy has an earlier set of high-level siamesed pipes that are lighter than the twin silencers fitted as standard, giving the bike a much slimmer look.*

OPPOSITE BOTTOM: *The timing side of the high-pipe TR6 looks bare without any exhaust. It serves to emphasize the slimness of Triumph's design.*

would endure until the end of the range of big Triumph twins. The USA saw two TR6 models: the Trophy Road Sports (TR6R) with large fuel tank and low pipes, and the TR6C Trophy Competition with slimline fuel tank and high pipes, one on each side. The road-oriented TR6R fuel tank was finished in Pacific Blue over Alaskan White and had white mudguards with gold stripe, while the TR6C slimline fuel tank was finished overall in Pacific Blue with a central Alaskan White racing stripe, with stainless steel mudguards. The only model made for the UK market was the TR6 Trophy with low pipes, again finished in Pacific Blue over Alaskan White tank, and white mudguards with a gold stripe.

For 1967 the USA saw Trophy Road Sports (TR6R) with low pipes, and TR6C Trophy Competition with high pipes, with two silencers mounted on the drive side. There were small oval bolt-on heat shields on the exhaust pipes

to protect the driver's legs, but no protection for a passenger. Both models were finished in Mist Green over white with stainless guards for the TR6C, and Mist Green painted guards for the TR6R. For the UK the TR6 Trophy had low pipes and was again finished in Mist Green over white.

The 1968 model year saw the US model TR6R and TR6C, and the UK model TR6. The US-market Trophy Sports (TR6R) had low pipes, and the TR6C Trophy Special had high pipes, both on the drive side, with small solid chromed head guards for the rider's leg. The TR6C's pipes were linked with an 'H' piece from April 1968 to quieten the bike down in the light of impending noise legislation in the USA. The TR6R's fuel tank was painted in Riviera Blue over silver, with Riviera Blue mudguards. The TR6C's fuel tank was overall Riviera Blue with a central racing silver stripe and its mudguards were stainless steel. The UK

This 1970 TR6 has a non-standard paint job but uses the Triumph-style scallops on the US-specification small tank to produce a superb effect.

TR6 Trophy fuel tank was finished in Riviera Blue and silver, with Riviera Blue guards.

The Tiger name was reintroduced to the USA in 1969 and applied to the road-oriented TR6R while the off-road oriented TR6C retained the Trophy name. The USA saw the TR6R Tiger with low pipes and the TR6C Trophy Special with high pipes, both routed over the primary drive and now protected with a new chromed wire heat guard nicknamed the 'chip basket' in the UK and the 'barbeque grill' in the USA – reflecting the different countries' cultures! The new heat guard ran roughly from the centre of the clutch to the rear shock and at last gave pretty good protection to the pillion passenger's leg.

The TR6R Tiger's 3½ US gallon fuel tank and mudguards were painted in Hi-Fi Red. The

TR6C Trophy's 2½ US gallon fuel tank was also finished in Hi-fi Red and its mudguards were polished stainless steel. For the UK market, there was just the road-oriented TR6 Trophy with low exhaust, very close in specification to the US specification Tiger, with its fuel tank and mudguards painted in Trophy Red.

The final year of the pre oil-in-frame models was 1970. The US models were the TR6R Tiger and the TR6C Trophy. As before the Tiger was equipped with low pipes and the TR6C Trophy Special with high pipes. Both were finished in Spring Gold (a greenish shade), with the Tiger having a wide black stripe on the centreline of the tank, and the TR6C having a somewhat narrower stripe. It appears that some bikes did not have the stripe at all. The TR6C had polished stainless steel mudguards, while

ABOVE: *The 1970 TR6 sported twin silencers on high-level pipes, with the famous 'chip basket' or 'barbeque grill' heat shield.*

RIGHT: *This 1966 US-specification TR6 has the correct high-level exhaust, the optional VDO speedometer and the small US tank. Spotted at the Fleet Lions run in May 2008.*

the Tiger had painted guards in Spring Gold, with a black stripe down the middle. The UK just had the TR6 Trophy Sports, with its tank and mudguards finished in Spring Gold.

Pre Oil-in-Frame Trophy and Tiger				
	1963 Trophy UK TR6S/S	*1963 Trophy US TR6/R/TR6/C*	*1967 Tiger TR6R/ Trophy TR6C*	*1970 Tiger TR6R/ Trophy TR6C/*
Engine				
Bore/stroke (mm)	71 × 82	71 × 82	71 × 82	71 × 82
Capacity (cc)	649	649	649	649
Compression ratio	8.5:1	8.5:1	9:1	9:1
Power (bhp @ rpm)	40 @ 6,500	45 @ 6,500	45 @ 6,500	45 @ 6,500
Carburettor				
Type	Amal Monobloc	Amal Monobloc	Amal Monobloc	Amal Concentric Mk1
Specification	376/285	376/40	389/97	930
Number	1	1	1	1
Transmission				
Engine sprocket (teeth)	29	29	29	29
Clutch sprocket (teeth)	58	58	58	58
Gearbox sprocket (teeth)	19 (sidecar 17)	19/18	19/18	19/18
Rear sprocket (teeth)	46	46	46	46
RPM, 10mph top gear	630	630/670	634/666	634/666
Gear ratios				
Fifth	–	–	–	–
Fourth	4.84:1	4.84 (5.12):1	4.84 (5.12):1	4.84 (5.11):1
Third	5.76:1	5.76 (6.08):1	5.76 (6.56):1	5.76 (6.09):1
Second	8.17:1	8.17 (8.64):1	8.17 (10.18):1	8.17:(8.63):1
First	11.81:1	11.81 (12.48):1	11.81 (13.41):1	11.81 (12.46):1
Wheels and tyres				
Front – size	3.25 × 19	3.25 × 19	3.25 × 18	3.25 × 18
Rear – size	4.00 × 18	4.00 × 18	4.00 × 18	3.50 × 18
Front brake	8in SLS drum	8in SLS drum	8in SLS drum (flanged hub)	8in TLS drum
Rear brake	7in SLS drum	7in SLS drum	7in SLS drum	7in SLS drum
Dimensions				
Seat height	30½in (77.5cm)	30½in (77.5cm)	30½in (77.5cm)	30½in (77.5cm)
Wheelbase	55½in (141cm)	55½in (141cm)	55½in (141cm)	55½in (141cm)
Length	84½in (214.5cm)	84½in (214.5cm)	84½in (214.5cm)	84½in (214.5cm)
Width	27in (68.5cm)	27in (68.5cm)	27in (68.5cm)	27in (68.5cm)
Ground clearance	5in (12.7cm)	5in (12.7cm)	7⅛in (18cm)	7⅛in (18cm)
Weight	363lb (165kg)	363lb (165kg)	363lb (165kg)/ 360lb (163kg)	369lb (167kg)
Fuel capacity	4gal (18ltr)	3gal (13.5ltr)	2½gal (11ltr)	4gal (18ltr)
Oil capacity	5 pints (2.8ltr)	5 pints (2.8ltr)	6 pints (3.4ltr)	6 pints (3.4ltr)

Twin-Carb Tearaways: T120, 1963–70

The T120 Bonneville was the sports model of the 1960s in both the UK and the USA. The model was introduced in pre-unit form in 1959 and replaced the T110 as the top sports model in the Triumph range. The Bonneville's 'trademark' was twin carburettors: no Bonneville left the factory with a single carburettor head, and the unit-construction T120 retained the splayed ports seen on the pre-unit model; these meant the carburettors were angled outwards on each side of the head, which helped gas flow, but also meant it was obvious that there were two carburettors – and that implied performance. Compare this setup with the contemporary Norton 650SS and BSA A65 Lightning, or even the 1968 Norton Commando. The Norton had parallel inlet ports, so the twin carburettors were really not very obvious, and the Lightning, even though it was equipped with splayed ports, did its best to hide its carburettors under bulbous side panels. As above, the following paragraphs describe the main details of the T120 models produced between 1963 and 1970.

On its introduction in 1963 the Bonneville was quite close in specification and appearance to the other bikes in the range, apart from the twin carburettors. It shared the same frame, wheels and brakes, but featured 8.5:1 compression-ratio pistons and twin Amal 376 Monobloc carburettors (types 286 and 287), which, in contrast to those fitted to the 1965 BSA A65 Lightning, were handed so a rider could actually tickle them.

The speedometer was still driven off the gearbox lay-shaft as on the pre-unit bikes, and there was a tachometer drive provided off the end of the exhaust camshaft. The tachometer drive was taken directly from the end of the exhaust camshaft, which meant the cable was screwed directly into the crankcases and then had to be bent through 90 degrees to snake its way up to the tachometer. This resulted in either a large loop of cable if directed outside of the exhaust pipe, which was vulnerable to snagging, or a very tight loop to pass the cable inside of the pipes, which shortened the life of the cable considerably. This unsatisfactory system was replaced in 1966 by the small gearbox, which turned the drive through 90 degrees only and reduced the gearing from direct to 2:1.

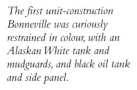

The first unit-construction Bonneville was curiously restrained in colour, with an Alaskan White tank and mudguards, and black oil tank and side panel.

The Bonneville engine design was closely based on the pre-unit motor, including the combustion chamber shape, valve angle and camshaft form. While the camshafts were designated E4819 inlet and E4855 exhaust cams, the inlet was in fact the famous E3134 profile but with a hollow centre for the engine breather, and the exhaust was the E3325 profile with an extension on its timing end to provide the contact-breaker drive and a tachometer drive fitting on the other end. This approach meant minimal design and development issues, leaving the designers free to concentrate on the 'unitization' of the motor.

The overall look of the Bonneville kept to the traditional Triumph sportster appearance: no unit Bonnie ever had enclosures fitted as standard, and the tight, clean Triumph line produced

LEFT: *The unit Bonneville matured into a fine machine. This US-specification 1969 model has the small 2½ gallon tank, with the famous Triumph 'scallop' paint job in red and silver.*

BELOW: *The author's 1970 T120R has a non-standard paint job, but is otherwise 99 per cent standard. It's a pleasure to ride and easy to work on.*

by Edward Turner and Triumph's chief stylist Jack Wickes was very much in evidence.

The Bonneville was produced in T120 guise for the UK and general export market, and in T120R (Road) and T120C (Competition) models for the US market, which was significant enough by 1963 to justify the production of specific models. The T120 featured a 4 gallon fuel tank, while the slimmer tanks fitted to the US T120R and T120C carried 3 gallons. The US models had fatter (4.00 section) rear tyres, and the Competition models also featured lower gearing, the ratios being the same as those supplied for sidecar use in the UK (Triumph rarely missed a trick when it came to saving money by using common components). US East Coast competition models tended to have high-level exhaust pipes, silencers and lights, and were fully road legal, while US West Coast variants were more radical with straight-through high-level pipes and no lights, so could not be used on the road legally. Interestingly, the US brochure claims all T120 models gave 50bhp, while the UK models in the same state of tune could only muster a claimed 46bhp – probably the West Coast T120C did achieve the full 50bhp with its lack of silencing!

The development of the Bonneville was fairly straightforward. The pre oil-in-frame T120 was gradually improved year on year, and it is generally considered to have been perfected during the last three years of production, 1968 to 1970. With the modified frame, excellent TLS front brake and the engine improvements giving increased performance and reliability, the Bonnie had evolved into a great machine.

For 1964 the Bonneville gained new footrests, fitted to the rear engine plates to increase ground clearance, and the external spring front forks. While the UK had the roadster T120, there were a number of sports models for the USA: the East and West Coast T120R road models, similar to the UK road version with low exhausts, and the T120C models. The 'C' models came in two flavours, both designated

The Bonneville's classic engine sports twin carbs on splayed-out ports. The later models had linked exhaust systems that gave less noise with no power loss.

T120C. The 'Competition Sports' variant for the East Coast was a road-legal scrambles bike, with lights and a high-level exhaust system with a pipe and a silencer on each side of the bike. The T120C 'TT Special', an out-and-out racer with no lights or silencers, is described separately below. Colours for the UK and US markets were Gold over Alaskan White fuel tank, black lining, and Alaskan White guards with a gold centre stripe. All lining between the two colours was in black.

The 1965 season saw the same range of bikes, in both road and competition variants as 1964. Colours were Pacific Blue over Silver on the fuel tank and silver mudguards with Pacific Blue stripe; all lining was in gold. The TT models' mudguards were polished alloy.

This 1970 UK-specification Bonneville features the large 4 gallon fuel tank – a practical touch for the UK market when bikes were still used for serious transport rather than just as leisure vehicles. It's a shame that Triumph did not give the bike the US-style paint job with the scallops as it would have improved the looks no end!

The 1966 season again saw no significant change in the range of bikes, with both road and competition variants as 1965. The year did see the introduction of the best-looking Triumph/BSA corporate rear light unit on the US models: a slim cast alloy unit carrying the Lucas 679 'teat' type lens. Colours were Grenadier Red over Alaskan White fuel tank for the UK models, and White guards with Grenadier Red stripe, and gold lining. The US bikes had the same finish for their mudguards but their fuel tanks were painted in Grenadier Red overall with White 'racing stripes' across the top of the tank. The East Coast TT models' mudguards were painted, the West Coast models were polished alloy.

The Bonneville range started to contract in 1967, when the UK T120 and US T120R road models were complemented by just one TT model. The colours for the UK market models were Aubergine over Alaskan White with white-striped Aubergine mudguards. The US models, both T120R and TT, had Aubergine over Gold fuel tanks and stainless steel polished mudguards. The T120R also lost the tank-top parcel grid.

By 1968 the Bonneville had arguably reached its zenith. Doug Hele's improvements to the frame and forks had given it world-class handling and roadholding, and the steady refinements to the engine had improved both performance and reliability. The final piece in

ABOVE: By 1968 the Bonneville was reaching its zenith. This nice clean model was at the Fleet Lions run in May 2008.

RIGHT: The Bonneville had a speedo and tacho as standard, fixed to a plate that was rubber-mounted on the fork yoke. This 1968 model shows the red and silver paint job and the steering damper positioned behind the handlebar mounts.

the jigsaw was the front brake, new for 1968: the big 8in (20.3cm) twin leading shoe unit finally gave the Bonneville the ability to stop as quickly as it went. Even the looks hit the spot, with the US specification fuel tank emphasizing the slim, lithe lines that made the bike look fast when it was standing still. The UK Bonnie sported a Hi-Fi Scarlet over silver 4 gallon fuel tank and silver-painted mudguards, while the US specification model had a Hi-Fi Scarlet tank with a silver central stripe, and polished stainless steel mudguards.

The 1969 model year saw few changes from 1968. The main colour of the bikes was Olympic Flame, an orangey red, and the UK bikes had this applied over silver on the fuel tank, with silver mudguards and a Olympic Flame stripe, all lined in gold. The year did see the introduction of Triumph's iconic 'scallop'

paint job in the US market. This style of finish was introduced during the model year, initially as two silver scallops sweeping back from the top of each tank badge, running over the top of the tank and tapering into a point at the seat nose, which contrasted brilliantly with the Olympic Flame base finish. Later that year, the design was complemented by the addition of a second scallop sweeping down from the bottom of the tank badge back to the knee rubbers.

The final year for the pre oil-in-frame Bonnie was 1970. Very similar to the 1969 bike, the main recognition feature is the front engine plate. The mudguards for both markets were finished in Astral Red with a silver stripe. The UK bikes' fuel tanks were Astral Red with a silver side panel, while the US models had the much more glamorous silver scallops.

The 1970 Bonneville in UK specification looks pretty good and goes well.

	Pre Oil-in-Frame T120 Bonneville			
	1963 Bonneville T120 (UK)	*1963 Bonneville T120R/T120C (US)*	*1967 Bonneville T120R*	*1970 Bonneville T120 US*
Engine				
Bore/stroke (mm)	71 × 82	71 × 82	71 × 82	71 × 82
Capacity (cc)	649	649	649	649
Compression ratio	8.5:1	8.5:1	9:1	
Power (bhp @ rpm)	46 @ 6,500	50 @ 6,500	50 @ 6,500 (with straight-through pipes)	52 @ 6,500
Carburettor				
Type	Amal Monobloc	Amal Monobloc	Amal Monobloc	Amal Concentric
Specification	376/286 – 287	376/286 – 287	389/95	930
Number	2	2	2	2
Transmission				
Engine sprocket (teeth)	29	29	29	29
Clutch sprocket (teeth)	58	58	58	58
Gearbox sprocket (teeth)	19	19/18	19	19
Rear sprocket (teeth)	46	46	46	46
RPM, 10 mph top gear	648	630/670	634	634
Gear ratios				
Fifth	–	–	–	–
Fourth	4.84:1	4.84 (5.12):1	4.84:1	4.84:1
Third	5.76:1	5.76 (6.08):1	5.76:1	5.76:1
Second	8.17:1	8.17 (8.64):1	8.17:1	8.17:1
First	11.81:1	11.81 (12.48):1	11.81:1	11.81:1
Wheels and tyres				
Front – size	3.25 × 19	3.25 × 19	3.25 × 19	3.25 × 19
Rear – size	3.50 × 18	4.00 × 18	4.00 × 18	4.00 × 18
Front brake	8in SLS	8in SLS	8in SLS (flanged hub)	8in TLS
Rear brake	7in SLS	7in SLS	7in SLS	7in SLS
Dimensions				
Seat height	30½in (77.5cm)	30½in (77.5cm)	30½in (77.5cm)	30½in (77.5cm)
Wheelbase	55in (139.6cm)	55¼in (140.3cm)	55in (139.6cm)	55½in (141cm)
Length	84in (213.5cm)	84½in (214.6cm)	84in (213.5cm)	84½in (214.6cm)
Width	27in (68.5cm)	27in (68.5cm)	27in (68.5cm)	27in (68.5cm)
Ground clearance	5in (12.7cm)	5in (12.7cm)	7⅛in (18.1cm)	7⅛in (18.1cm)
Weight	363lb (165kg)	363lb (165kg)	363lb (165kg)	386lb (175kg)
Fuel capacity	4gal (18ltr)	3gal (13.5ltr)	2½gal (11ltr)	2½gal (11ltr)
Oil capacity	5 pints (2.8ltr)	5 pints (2.8ltr)	6 pints (3.4ltr)	6 pints (3.4ltr)

Stop Anything in No Time: Saint Police Bikes

The Thunderbird formed the basis for Triumph's 650cc offerings to numerous UK and foreign police forces up until the introduction of the Trophy-based TR6P Saint in 1966, and a separate catalogue for police bikes was available from 1965. Triumphs were always popular with London's Metropolitan Police (the 'Met') and many UK police forces followed the Met's lead when ordering machines. Essentially Triumph would supply what a force wanted, usually a standard Thunderbird with white tank and mudguards, single seat and radio carrier. The individual police forces would then fit leg shields or fairings and any other equipment needed.

The Thunderbird-based police models had a number of changes to the standard bike and also incorporated a number of TR6 Trophy components. The following list, taken from the official Triumph Replacement Part Catalogue for 1966 Police Thunderbird models (from engine DU6547), summarizes the changes to the stock Thunderbird model:

- Pistons and rings (the bottom end of the engine was all TR6 from 1964)
- Crankcase chain oiler assembly
- Cylinder head

The Saint was based on the 6T and, after 1966, the TR6. Note the fairing and panniers.

- Gearbox sprocket and Speedo drive gears
- RM20 alternator stator (higher output stator)
- Centre stand (two return springs), to handle the weight of all the additional equipment
- Rear sub-frame, adapted to carry single seat
- Exhaust pipes and silencers
- Nacelle top, 30 amp ammeter, horn and wiring harness
- Petrol tank and additional rubber mountings for radio
- Battery (Lucas SCZ7E), rectifier and battery carrier (note that the 'standard' model was still 6 volt)
- Chronometric speedometer – certified, available calibrated in mph or km/h.

In addition to these 'standard' items there was a range of alternative equipment that customers could order. This list included:

- Twin seat and radio carrier
- Battery carrier for 12 volt system, including twin 6 volt batteries
- 12 volt electrical conversion kit including stator (RM19), coil, zener diode and heat sink, horn, bulbs and wiring loom
- Aerial mounting bracket, including a special rear mudguard drilled to accept the bracket
- Crash bar and fittings
- Leg shields and fittings
- Blue lamp – 5 inch (12.7cm) diameter Lucas L724 and mounts.

LEFT: *The single carburettor and special tune gave the Saint excellent performance up to around 100mph.*

BELOW: *A radio could be fitted in a well in the fuel tank, as in this example. The specially calibrated Smiths chronometric speedometer was mounted on a TR6-style bracket – the tacho was an extra cost option.*

Ex-police Thunderbird models are easily identified: up to 1964 they have the prefix 6TW, but from then onwards police bikes were prefixed 6TP, a more meaningful designation.

As police forces became more sophisticated in developing their own requirements in the early 1960s, Triumph had to become more proactive in the design and development of models designed specifically for the police. When the Thunderbird ceased production in 1966, Triumph did not want to lose the relatively lucrative police market. Following on from earlier developments, the single-carburettor TR6 Trophy model became the basis for a Police model that gained the name 'Saint' (Stop Anything in No Time).

The Saint was never a 'standard' bike as such, since Triumph would produce whatever each individual police force wanted. However, the basic specification and tune of the bike was standardized. The engine was a standard TR6, apart from a new cylinder head, large bore single carburettor, wide ratio gearbox (for 1970 models) and low (7.5:1) compression ratio pistons. The Saint was renowned for its mixture of tractability, rapid acceleration from rest and a top speed in excess of 100mph (160km/h); all of the Saints supplied to the Metropolitan Police were individually tested by the Motor Industry Research Association (MIRA) and certified as achieving a top speed of more than 100mph before delivery.

The Saints' engine and frame numbers were prefixed TR6P. Such ex-police models were sought after in the 1970s because of their balanced performance, despite the fact that it could be a bit of a lottery to get one that was in good condition. The Saints were well maintained but were sold off 'as seen' when they were officially no longer needed: lucky buyers might get one that had just had a big service or a reconditioned engine, but unlucky buyers got one that was just in need of a replacement motor.

Competition in the USA: T120TT

The Triumph Bonneville T120TT owed nothing to the Isle of Man, but everything to the US sport of oval racing – short courses where big bikes race on shingle. The US TT Steeplechase race formula differed from the oval circuit short-track, half-mile and one-mile events in that it featured both right- and left-hand turns and one or more jumps. The bikes used on this type of race would be fitted with front brakes, unlike those used for oval circuit racing. This was a spectacular and hard sport for which Triumph 650s, with their good power and tractability, were ideally suited. So for 1963 Triumph introduced a specialized model based on the Bonneville, the T120TT, to give the US racers an 'out of the box' racer. These bikes were not just used for racing – the famous stunt rider Evel Knievel used one in his early days, including for his famous jump over the fountains at Caesar's Palace in Las Vegas, where he memorably crashed, breaking his pelvis, hip and ribs, but assured his reputation.

The Triumph T120TT was produced from 1963 through to 1967, but disappeared from the listings for the 1968 model year. It was produced for the US market only and was never marketed in the UK or general export market. The bike was a stripped-down and hopped-up T120 Bonneville. Its engine was in a much higher state of tune than the standard T120, and it had no lighting or silencing. Its trademark in its later years was the two exhaust pipes that swept down under the engine, terminating under the gearbox housing. While they encroached on the bike's ground clearance, this was not important on the shingle TT tracks where cornering clearance was more important, and they certainly increased the bike's ability to lean!

The first TT model, introduced to the USA early in 1963, was produced by Meriden specifically at the request of the Triumph US West Coast distributor Johnson Motors. It was a tuned Bonneville with all the road equipment stripped off and an engine giving (claimed) 52bhp (2bhp greater than the standard Bonneville). The engine tuning featured a 12:1 compression ration. When the bike was tested by *Cycle World* magazine it turned in a top speed of 123.5mph (198.7km/h), with the engine revving up to 7,900rpm, with no apparent ill effects. Delivered without lights or battery, but with 'AC magneto' (also known as energy transfer) ignition and with high-level pipes substituted for a

low-level set used in the test, the bike was otherwise the same as the 1963 Bonneville, finished in Alaskan White and with painted steel mudguards.

The 1964 model was described in the Triumph literature, with Triumph's emphasis, just as it appeared in the brochure, as being for 'the Competition Expert who wants top performance with Twin Carburettors, *without lighting equipment*, etc., and *primarily for off the road, racing*

RIGHT: The TT was first listed in the 1964 brochure. The bike was an out and out off-road racer with a high-level exhaust and no lights or other road equipment.

BELOW: The 1967 brochure shows the T120TT as a mean and purposeful racer. The exhaust pipes were led under the engine for maximum ground clearance.

and competition use'. The bike was based on the Bonneville and, like the 1963 TT model, featured the road bike's frame and running gear.

Specialized racing equipment included AC magneto ignition, aluminium alloy mudguards, no lights, battery and speedometer, and a high-level exhaust system with long pipes, sweeping up over the crankcases on both sides, that extended to just behind the line of the rear-wheel spindle. No silencers were fitted, and there was a small solid head shield on each pipe to protect the rider's leg. No pillion pegs or centre stand were fitted. The engine was still heavily tuned, but sported a slightly lower compression ratio than 1963 at 11.2:1, in comparison to the standard 1964 Bonneville's 8.5:1, and had twin 1⁵⁄₁₆in Amal Monobloc carburettors (while the standard 1964 Bonneville had smaller 1⅛in Monoblocs).

In its 1964 brochure for the US market, Triumph quoted the May 1963 issue of *Cycle World* in which its Technical Editor described achieving 123.5mph over a drag of three-quarters of a mile (1.2km) on a 1963 TT model related to a 1963 'JoMo' model with its slightly higher tuned engine.

The TT was listed from 1963 to 1967, when it retained its high state of tune and benefited from the detailed changes made to the rest of the range. Its colour scheme was the same as the Bonneville, but for 1964 and 1965 the bike featured unpainted alloy mudguards. For 1966 East Coast models had painted mudguards (white with a red stripe), while West Coast models retained the alloys. For the last year of production, 1967, unpainted stainless steel guards were fitted. The trademark TT exhaust pipes, 1¾in (4.5cm) diameter items that swept down under the crankcases and terminated just in front of the rear wheel, were introduced in 1965 and

The Thruxton Bonneville was named after the circuit in Hampshire that hosted the annual 500-mile endurance race. This is Dave Degans on a Thruxton at Castle Combe in July 1965, when he and Barry Lawton won the 500-mile event.

were fitted until the end of production in 1967. The TT was a pure racing machine and enjoyed considerable success in the USA.

Competition in the UK: Thruxton Bonneville

In contrast to the US market TT Bonneville, the other sports model produced by Triumph was the road sports-oriented Thruxton Bonneville, named after the racing circuit near Andover, Hampshire, where Triumph had great success in the Thruxton 500-mile endurance races in the 1960s.

The Thruxton was produced in limited numbers by Triumph to justify its 'production racer' status and was firmly based on the T120. The first models appeared in 1964, when just eight were produced. Production was stepped up for 1965, with fifty-two models being produced. The last year of production was 1966, when the few examples then produced were retained by the factory. The modifications from standard were surprisingly few. The main mechanical modification was a positive oil feed to the exhaust camshaft. This was an internal feed on the 1964 machines and external on the 1965 machines, with an oil pipe running from the timing side to the tappet block in the barrel.

Other changes included 8.5:1 pistons, a new cylinder head with larger exhaust valves,

The Thruxton was a limited edition machine, designed and produced in the Triumph competition shop for production racing.
It was recognizably based on the standard production Bonneville.

stronger 'red spot' valve springs, a separate external float chamber for the twin chopped 1⅛in Amal Monobloc carburettors, different gear ratios, a modified frame with fairing mounts, rear-set footrests, racing seat, alloy wheel rims and a new free-flow exhaust system – with the silencers having a flat bracing strip to support their ends. Some oil tanks and side panels were produced with cut-outs to allow long bell mouths to be fitted to the carburettors. Despite the relatively long list of modifications, the Thruxton was still recognizably based on the production machines and contributed significantly to the Bonneville's mystique. The Thruxton was an extremely successful production racer and the culmination

of its career was the first 100mph (160km/h) lap of the Isle of Man TT course by a production machine in 1969 (*see* Chapter 6).

Competition in the USA: 750cc T120RT

Triumph's position on the US sporting scene had been well established by the late 1960s with many successes in the American Motorcyclist Association (AMA) dirt racing series. There was a big change in 1969, however, when the AMA changed the capacity rules, allowing production-based machines of up to 750cc to be raced. This left Triumph in a dilemma. Their 750cc Trident was too big and heavy to be truly competitive on the dirt, and the popular and competitive 650cc twins were 100cc down against the opposition. The factory had no plans to increase the capacity of the twins at that time, as they viewed the Trident as the way ahead, which it was with great potential in road racing. To conform to AMA rules, a bike had to be a production model and be listed and available to the public before it would be allowed onto the race track. In addition, at least 200 of the model had to have been made. Triumph homologated just such a model in 1970, with the introduction of the T120RT, but the actual 'production' of the 200 T120RT bikes was carried out by the race shop of Tricor, Triumph's US East Coast distributor in Baltimore (145 bikes) and by the West Coast distributor at Durate, California (55 bikes). An additional four bikes were also produced, including the Tricor prototype. In order to produce a 750cc twin, Tricor went down the easiest route of fitting a new set of big bore barrels and new pistons onto the 204 standard 650cc T120R Bonnevilles while they were still crated up. The conversion involved only nine parts – the barrel, two pistons, piston rig set, gudgeon pin circlips, cylinder head and base gaskets, socket-headed centre head bolt with new washer, tappet feed plug and a new cylinder base gasket – and the kits were supplied by Sonny Routt, a well-known US supplier of good-quality Triumph tuning parts. The cylinder barrel was made in cast iron and was very similar in appearance to the standard Triumph item. Those supplied also had the corners on the bottom of the barrel radiused to closely resemble the Triumph part. The only giveaway was the two 'Motor Castings' logos (a small 'c' inside a larger 'M', both enclosed in an upside down triangle) on the base flange by the tappet blocks. The Tricor part number (E6304-T7) was also stamped on the timing side of the forward face of the flange.

At the end of the operation each bike had a 'T' stamped after the 'T120R' stamp on the crankcases, hence the T120RT was born. David Gaylin, in his *Triumph Motorcycle Restoration Guide* (1997), states that only the engine number was stamped and that the frame prefix was left as T120R since it was not possible to get to the frame number with the bike still strapped down in its packing case.

The bikes were built up before June 1970 from 1970-model Bonnevilles so all had the removable front engine plates. A Triumph Service Bulletin was issued on 30 June 1970 describing the 'Bonneville 750'. This gives details of the parts that made up the kit and shows that the cylinders came bored to 76mm plus 0.008in, giving an actual bore of 76.02mm (or just under 3.0in) and a capacity of 744.4cc. There were also specified oversized pistons at +0.040in. These required the barrels to be rebored to 76.1mm (3.032in) and gave a slightly increased capacity of 746cc. One bike was assigned to each Triumph dealer in the US as a factory experimental unit for racing only – and buyers were asked to sign a disclaimer to that effect. The factory only found out about the existence of the T120RT when an order for a large number of crankshafts was put in from the US: racers were taking no chances with the 750cc RTs and were rebuilding them with new crankshafts much more often than was normal (it is rumoured that some were changing the crank every other race). Despite this, the 750cc RTs had an impressive number of wins in the early 1970s.

As a postscript to the RT tale, while most of the bikes were raced, some remained in captivity and were used as everyday rides. One such bike was owned by Pat Owens, who was the Johnson Motors Service Manager at Durate. He bought the first T120RT converted at Durate and had covered more than 400,000 miles (644,000km) on it by 1993, when it still had its original crankcases, cylinder head, valve seats and most of the transmission – a fine tribute to the strength of Triumph's fundamental design.

3 Model Development, 1971–88

Oil in Frame (OIF): the Last of the 650s and Introducing the 750s

For the 1971 season it was all change for the Triumph and BSA range. All of the 'B' series models' running gear – frame, forks, wheels and tinware – was replaced as a result of a major development programme carried out by the BSA development centre at Umberslade Hall. The Triumph 'B' series range comprised three bikes: the T120R Bonneville, with its twin carburettors, and two single-carburettor bikes, the 'off-road' (or rather 'high piped') TR6C Trophy 650, and the 'sensible' or on-road TR6R Tiger 650. All were fitted with an attractive 3½ US gallon rounded fuel tank.

The first oil-in-frame models tended to keep the Triumph look. This US-specification Tiger 650 has the 3 gallon rounded tank decked out in the traditional Triumph scallop paint job.

Apart from a non-standard paint colour and silencers, this 1971/72 Bonneville looks pretty standard. Note the conical hub and twin leading shoe front brake, fitted from 1971.

The new, all-welded frame, with its large diameter backbone tube carrying the oil, was complemented by new 'Ceriani' style front forks with alloy sliders and exposed chrome stanchions, and two-way damping. The wheels were all new, with steel rims, galvanized spokes and cast alloy conical hubs with shrunk-in steel brake linings. The front brake was an 8in (20.3cm) diameter twin leading shoe unit, while the rear wheel sported a 7in (17.8cm) diameter single leading shoe brake. Mudguards were also all new, with the front unit rubber-mounted on wire supports running fore and aft from the fork sliders. The range had high US-style handlebars (the same as fitted to the pre-OIF US models) and with their relatively short mudguards were described as 'chopper style' by the somewhat conservative UK press. Electrics were bought up to date, with new integrated switchgear on the handlebars, which incorporated high quality forged alloy control levers.

Indicators were fitted as standard, at last, and the instruments were placed in rubber pods that bolted to the fork top nuts via figure-of-eight shaped chromed mounts. The engines remained largely unchanged, apart from some modifications to the rocker boxes, which were needed to make them fit in the new frame.

T120R Bonneville, TR6C Trophy and TR6 Tiger

The 1971 model year Bonneville was supplied with the traditional twin carburettors, and the first models were fitted with a shapely curved 3 gallon fuel tank that resembled the pre-OIF models, but was mounted on large rubber saddles over the large diameter top tube and had the traditional BSA centre-bolt fixing.

The Bonneville had twin Amal Concentric 930 30mm choke carburettors while the Trophy and Tiger were, as usual, equipped with a single Amal Concentric 930. Otherwise the differences between the bikes were minimal. The single-carburettor models had a different air box to the Bonneville, with a central pipe linking the carburettor to the box, while the Bonneville's twin carburettors had separate rubber hoses linking each carburettor into the air box. All models had their air boxes/side panels finished in black.

Both the Tiger and Bonneville had low-level exhaust systems with new 'megaphone'-style silencers, one each side. While these looked good they were prone to splitting around the mounting plates that connected them to the rear footrest carriers.

A 7in (17.8cm) diameter flat-backed headlamp carried the pilot/main light switch and

ABOVE: The 1971 Bonneville came in gold and white. Later in the year UK versions were supplied with the 4 gallon 'bread bin' tank.

The 1971 TR6C Trophy, rare in the UK, was virtually identical to the Tiger, apart from its high-level exhaust system.

The 1971 TR6R Tiger was a single-carburettor roadster.

LEFT: The 1971 Bonneville had two separate side panels with the front finned cover carrying the air filter element. The standard gold paintwork with black scallops is nicely reproduced on this example.

BELOW LEFT: The 'Gargoyle' rear light included mounts for the standard indicators.

BELOW: The US-styled 3-gallon tank was a traditional Triumph shape, held a decent amount of fuel and looked good – so Triumph in its wisdom discontinued it in 1973. This is on a 1971 TR6C Trophy.

three warning lights (oil pressure, high beam and indicators). The ignition switch, which also operated the lights, was inconveniently positioned on the back of the right-hand side panel.

The 1971 Bonneville's fuel tank was finished in Spring Gold with black scallops (above and below the 'picture frame'-type tank badge) with white lining. The mudguards were also painted Spring Gold. The 1971 Trophy's fuel tank was finished in Pacific Blue with white scallops (above and below the 'picture frame'-type tank badge) with gold lining and the mudguards were painted Pacific Blue.

In keeping with its 'off-road' image, the Trophy was equipped with a high-level exhaust system similar to the previous year's, but with longer traditional Triumph cigar-style silencers, both mounted on the drive side. The 'chip basket' or 'barbeque grill' heat shield was fitted, and the longer silencers meant the tail pipes reached almost to the rear light.

The Trophy did not have a tachometer as standard, the headlamp was a 6in (15.2cm) diameter chromed unit, and a pressed steel sump guard and folding footrests were fitted, but otherwise it was identical to the Tiger. The 1971 Trophy's finish was the same as the Tiger, but the Trophy's mudguards were chromed.

Later on in the 1971 model year, the 4 gallon 'breadbin'-style tank was introduced on the Bonneville and Tiger models for the UK market; this initially had a cheap and nasty stick-on 'Triumph' badge. The late 1971 UK market Bonneville breadbox tank was painted Tiger Gold over black, with a black stripe over the top of the tank. The join between the black and the gold was lined in white and the mudguards were Tiger Gold. The Tiger's 4 Imperial gallon tank was painted Pacific Blue with a broad white stripe across the top.

All three of the 650cc bikes continued into 1972 largely unchanged apart from the modified

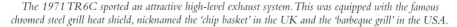

The 1971 TR6C sported an attractive high-level exhaust system. This was equipped with the famous chromed steel grill heat shield, nicknamed the 'chip basket' in the UK and the 'barbeque grill' in the USA.

LEFT: *The customizing possibilities with an OIF Triumph are endless. Here a restored 1971–73 Tiger 650cc is ready to take to the road. The paintwork is not standard but the bike looks lovely.*

BELOW: *A more radical approach to customizing an early OIF Bonneville: the popular flat-track look, with big rear tyre, minimalist lights, no indicators and a custom exhaust exploits the Triumph look.*

frame that brought the seat height down to a claimed 32in (81.3cm), and different paint schemes. The new five-speed gearbox was offered as an option for the Bonneville. The US-specification bikes retained the 3½ US gallon fuel tank, while the UK bikes had the 4 Imperial gallon breadbin type. The US bikes' paint scheme had a main colour over a white lower half, with black pinstriping delineating the two colours along the top of the tank badge

The last 650 twin (apart from the 1980s Thunderbird) was the 1974 T120V Bonneville.
This was virtually identical to the 750cc models, and came in Purple and White.

and the bottom of the knee indent: the Bonneville had Tiger Gold as its main colour, while the Tiger had Polychromatic Blue.

Both the Tiger and the Bonneville had their mudguards painted in their main colour. The Trophy had Polychromatic Blue as its main colour, but had chromed mudguards. The UK Bonneville and Tiger with the breadbin tank followed the US colour scheme, but with a straight line between the main colour and the white, running about three-quarters from the top of the tank.

The Trophy TR6C was dropped for 1973, while the Tiger TR6R and Bonneville T120R were overshadowed by the 750 models with the same names. The 1973 bikes were almost the last of the line for the 650cc twin, and were pretty much unchanged from the 1972 models. The Tiger TR6R was dropped at the end of the 1973 model year, being replaced by the TR7RV 750cc Tiger. The last 650cc T120V Bonnevilles were produced early in the 1974 season and were virtually identical to the 750 models, equipped with the 10in (25.4cm) Lockheed front disc brake as seen on the T140 and TR7RV and a five-speed gearbox. Both the UK and US T120V models had a purple fuel tank, with a Cold White panel lined in gold on the UK breadbin tank or a pair of Cold White scallops over the top of the US 2½ gallon tank.

Cylinder Head Stories: Nine and Ten Studs

The 650cc pre-unit Triumph cylinder head was fixed to the block using eight fixings, arranged around the cylinder bores. The introduction of the 650cc unit engine included a new cylinder head that incorporated a ninth fixing, a ⅜in bolt fitted between the two bores in the barrel, slightly to the front of the engine. This extra fixing complemented the other eight ⅜in diameter fixings, which were radially dispersed around the bores and helped to keep the head-to-block

Oil-in-Frame TR6R Tiger, TR6C Trophy and T120 Bonneville

	1971 Tiger TR6R / Trophy TR6C	1973 Tiger TR6R	1971 Bonneville T120R	1973 Bonneville T120V
Engine				
Bore/stroke (mm)	71 × 82	71 × 82	71 × 82	71 × 82
Capacity (cc)	649	649	649	649
Compression ratio	9:1	9:1	9:1	9:1
Power (bhp @ rpm)	Not given	Not given	Not given	Not given
Carburettor				
Type	Amal Concentric Mk1	Amal Concentric Mk1	Amal Concentric Mk1	Amal Concentric Mk1
Specification	930	930	R930 + L930	R930 + L930
Number	1	1	2	2
Transmission				
Engine sprocket (teeth)	29	29	29	29
Clutch sprocket (teeth)	58	58	58	58
Gearbox sprocket (teeth)	19	19	19	19
Rear sprocket (teeth)	47	47	47	47
RPM, 10 mph top gear	659 / 696	660	659	660
Gear ratios				
Fifth	–	–	–	4.90:1
Fourth	4.95 (5.22):1	4.95:1	4.95:1	5.89:1
Third	6.14 (6.48):1	6.14:1	6.14:1	6.92:1
Second	8.36 (8.83):1	8.36:1	8.36:1	9.09:1
First	12.08 (12.73):1	12.08:1	12.08:1	12.08:1
Wheels and tyres				
Front – size	3.25 × 19	3.25 × 19	3.25 × 19	3.25 × 19
Rear – size	4.00 × 18	4.00 × 18	4.00 × 18	4.00 × 18
Front brake	8in TLS drum	8in TLS drum	8in TLS drum	8in TLS drum Final versions had 10in disc
Rear brake	7in SLS drum	7in SLS drum	7in SLS drum	7in SLS drum
Dimensions				
Seat height	32in (81.3cm)	31in (79cm)	32in (81.3cm)	31in (79cm)
Wheelbase	56in (142.2cm)	56in (142.2cm)	56in (142.2cm)	56in (142.2cm)
Length	87½in (222cm)	87½in (222cm)	87½in (222cm)	87½in (222cm)
Width	33in (84cm)	29in (73.6cm)	33in (84cm)	29in (73.6cm)
Ground clearance	7in (17.8cm) / 7½in (19cm)	7in (17.8cm)	7½in (19cm)	7in (17.8cm)
Weight	385lb (174kg)/ 381lb (173kg)	386lb (175kg)	382lb (173kg)	387lb (175kg)
Fuel capacity	3½ gal (13.25ltr)/ 3 gal (11.4ltr) optional 4.8 gal (18.2ltr)	4 gal (18.2ltr)/ optional 2 gal (9.1ltr)	3½ gal (13.25ltr) optional 4.8 gal (18.2ltr)	4 gal (18.2ltr)/ optional 2 gal (9.1ltr)
Oil capacity	4 pints (2.25ltr) (claimed 5 pints)	4 pints (2.25ltr) (claimed 5 pints)	4 pints (2.25ltr) (claimed 5 pints)	4 pints (2.25ltr) (claimed 5 pints)

joint gas-tight, especially between the two bores where there is not a lot of metal.

This system worked well and there are no documented weaknesses of the head block joint. The design remained unchanged for the twelve-year life of the 650cc engine.

The drive from the US to get a 750cc-class twin led to the introduction of the T120RT, with its aftermarket big bore kit, which retained the 650cc nine-stud head. This modification did expose that the head-to-block sealing was a bit marginal with the reduced width between the bores, and development work by Triumph as they struggled to get the 750cc model to the market confirmed that the joint needed some engineering attention.

When the first 750cc models hit the market in September 1972 (during the 1973 model year) the bikes featured a bore and stroke of 75 × 82mm giving a capacity of 724cc. This was caused by the use of the original 650cc cylinder block casting, which could not be bored out to the full 76mm and still have any re-bore potential. However, the literature is unclear whether these early T140 and TR7s had the old nine-stud fixings or the ten-stud fixings from the start. All my sources are ambiguous, describing the introduction of the 724cc bikes, followed by the 744cc models, but then referring to the ten-stud head being fitted to the '750 models'.

Initial investigations using parts books and the literature showed the 724cc block had part number 71-3335 (mistyped in the 1973 parts manual as 71-33335) and was introduced at bike number JH15435 (T140V) and KH17122 (TR7RV). The full 744cc bikes with bore and stroke of 76 × 82mm were introduced in December 1972, with engine and frame number XH22019 (T140V) and AH23727 (TR7RV). Posts on the Internet merely confirmed that there was a lack of real evidence. Finally, talking to respected Triumph writer David Gaylin unearthed a road test of an early 724cc in the May 1973 edition of *Cycle World*, in which the pictures and technical description

show that a ten-stud head was fitted. This was backed up by a 1973 Triumph parts manual (part 99-0980 – even parts manuals have their own part numbers!), which showed a ten-stud head used with the modified 650 block. Verbal

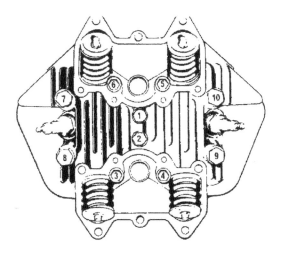

ABOVE: *The T140 cylinder head had an additional pair of studs between the bores, which replaced the single fixing used on the 650cc engine. This gave ten cylinder-head fixing studs in all. The new fixings are here labelled 1 and 2.*

BELOW: *The 1982 Royal features the 750cc ten-stud cylinder head. You can make out the two centre studs between the rocker boxes.*

confirmation also came from Rockerbox's resident mechanic, Arthur Frearson, that 'all the early 750 Triumphs used the ten-stud head'. Despite all the research I've carried out on this issue, there are inconsistencies in the Triumph literature: the first 750cc workshop manual identifies that the bore of the engines covered was 76mm but it claims that it covers from engine number KH17124, when most sources state that the 76mm bore was introduced later at XH22019. This only serves to demonstrate that it is doubly important in such a case not to trust any evidence unless it can be verified from more than one source – and make sure that different sources are independent.

So in conclusion, I can state with certainty that all of the 750cc Triumphs were equipped with ten-stud heads – until someone can prove otherwise!

The 750cc Revolution: T140V Bonneville

The introduction of the 750cc three-cylinder Trident into the Triumph range in 1968 gave the company a new 'superbike' to compete with the big bikes being introduced by the Japanese – most notably the four-cylinder 750cc Honda CB750.

While the factory saw the Trident as the natural successor to the Bonneville at the top of the range, and was reluctant to take the twin above 650cc, the market thought otherwise. The US market had been crying out for a 750cc twin for competition work from the end of the 1960s, which resulted in the semi-official T120RT being produced by Triumph's US East Coast distributor (*see* Chapter 2). While Bert Hopwood was still convinced that 650cc was the maximum practical size for a vertical twin, the market demanded a 750cc twin and the 750cc T140V was introduced in 1973.

As Hopwood described in his book *Whatever Happened to the British Motorcycle Industry* (1981), the production of the new 750cc twin was not just a case of boring the 650cc engine out and getting it to market, although the US distributors had done just that to produce the T120RT model. There were a number of problems with this simplistic approach, including crankshaft breakages, head gasket failures, oil leaks and unacceptable vibration, all of which

The first of the 750 Bonnies appeared in 1973. These had a disc front brake, drum rear and right-hand-side gear change. Note the silencers, only fitted in this year, with their curved endcaps.

ABOVE: *This early 1973/74 T140V shows the US-market styling, the drum rear brake and the right-foot gear change. Norton 'peashooter' silencers are a popular fitment to 750 Triumphs.*

BELOW: *From 1976 Triumph twins had left-foot gear change and disc rear brake. Here is a 1976/77 model with the US peanut tank.*

had to be engineered out before the unit could be cleared for production.

The new T140V Bonneville used the oil-in-frame running gear of the T120R, but was fitted as standard with the Triumph Lockheed front hydraulic disc brake. The bike was supplied in either UK or US variants, the US variant having a new small 2½ US gallon peanut tank painted in Vermilion (a bright metallic red) with a gold scallop, lined in white and a new higher bend handlebar. The UK version had the 4 Imperial gallon breadbin tank, rubber gaiters on the front forks and low bars, again finished in Vermilion with a gold panel that extended back over the top of the rubber knee grips on the side of the tank. Mudguards were chromed and were longer than the ones fitted to the 650 models, giving better weather protection. The front guard also reverted to the 1970 style of stays, with the front two loops connecting to the fixing at the top of the sliders and one running round the back of the guard and fixing to the

axle caps on the bottom of the fork sliders. This provided the front forks with extra rigidity and fixed the problem of the forks twisting under heavy breaking. A new left-hand side handlebar switch operated the horn, flasher, dip and main and indicators, and meant a switch back to cheap pressed steel brake and clutch levers. The Bonneville was largely unchanged for 1974, apart from the inevitable colour change, which only affected the petrol tank as chromed mudguards were standard and side panels were black. The 1974 Bonneville had the fuel tank painted Cherokee Red as the main colour with gold-lined Cold White scallops on the US tank and Cold White side panels on the UK breadbin. The Meriden sit-in brought production of 1974 models to a halt in October 1973 and it did not restart until 1975, when the Co-op started assembling the remaining stock of 1974 models.

Changes to US legislation meant that the 1976 Bonneville had to have its gear change moved from the right-hand side to the left. This

Triumph's 1978 T140RV model was painted Tawny Brown and Gold, with a brown seat. This was not a popular colour combination.

ABOVE: Nick Vale's 1977 US-specification T140V Bonneville. Mostly standard apart from the silencers, it shows the US style.

RIGHT: The T140V engine is instantly recognizable as a Triumph. The splayed head emphasizes the twin carbs.

required a new gear lever positioned in the middle of the primary chain case, connected to the gear-change mechanism by a spindle that ran inside the crankcases ahead of the gearbox across the engine.

The left-foot gear change meant that the foot brake also had to be moved and Triumph took the opportunity to fit a hydraulically operated disc. The type chosen was slightly thinner (0.235in/5.96mm) than that previously fitted at the front (0.25in/6.35mm), and the thinner disk was standardized front and rear, as was the calliper. The bike continued largely unchanged in this form into 1977, apart from the paintwork, and was eventually replaced by the T140E in 1978.

The Sensible 750: TR7RV Tiger

The 750cc TR7RV Tiger was introduced at the same time as the 750cc Bonneville, to which it was identical apart from its cylinder head, single carburettor, air cleaner assembly, badges and paint. The bike was promoted as the softer touring bike in the range and, with its single carburettor, it was more flexible but had less power in the top end than the Bonneville.

LEFT: *The 750cc TR7RV Tiger was introduced in 1973. This Canadian model shows the drum rear brake and the high export handlebars, new for 1973. Note the lack of a calliper cover on this brochure shot.*

BELOW: *The TR7RV Tiger was the single-carburettor tourer in the range. TR7RVs made between 1974 and 1977 were finished in Sea Jade Green with Ice White highlights – just the pattern changed.*

TR7RV Tiger, T140V and T140E Bonneville				
	1973 Tiger TR7RV	*1973 Bonneville T140V*	*1979 Tiger TR7 (UK Only)*	*1979 Bonneville T140E*
Engine				
Bore/stroke (mm)	75 × 82 to XH22018 then 76 × 82	75 × 82 to XH22018 then 76 × 82	76 × 82	76 × 82
Capacity (cc)	724 to XH22018 then 744	724 to XH22018 then 744	744	744
Compression ratio	8.5:1	8.5:1	7.9:1	7.9:1
Power (bhp @ rpm)	Not given	Not given	Not given	Not given
Carburettor				
Type	Amal Concentric Mk1	Amal Concentric Mk1	Amal Concentric Mk1	Amal Concentric Mk2
Specification	930	930	930	2930
Number	1	2	1	2
Transmission				
Engine sprocket (teeth)	29	29	29	29
Clutch sprocket (teeth)	58	58	58	58
Gearbox sprocket (teeth)	20	20	20	20
Rear sprocket (teeth)	47	47	47	47
RPM, 10mph top gear	634	634	627	627
Gear ratios				
Fifth	4.70:1	4.70:1	4.70:1	4.70:1
Fourth	5.59:1	5.59:1	5.59:1	5.59:1
Third	6.58:1	6.58:1	6.58:1	6.58:1
Second	8.63:1	8.63:1	8.63:1	8.63:1
First	12.15:1	12.15:1	12.14:1	12.14:1
Wheels and tyres				
Front – size	3.25 × 19	3.25 × 19	4.10 × 19	4.10 × 19
Rear – size	4.00 × 18	4.00 × 18	4.10 × 18	4.10 × 18
Front brake	10in (254 mm) disc	10in (254mm) disc	10in (254 mm) disc	10in (254 mm) disc
Rear brake	7in SLS drum	7in SLS drum	7in SLS drum	7in SLS drum
Dimensions				
Seat height	31in (79cm)	31in (79cm)	31in (79cm)	31in (79cm)
Wheelbase	56in (142.2cm)	56in (142.2cm)	56in (142.2cm)	56in (142.2cm)
Length	87½in (222cm)	87½in (222cm)	87½in (222cm)	87½in (222cm)
Width	29in (73.6cm)	29in (73.6cm)	27in (68.6cm) US 31in (83.8cm)	27in (68.6cm) US bars 31in (83.8cm)
Ground clearance	7in (17.8cm)	7in (17.8cm)	7in (17.8cm)	7in (17.8cm)
Weight	389lb (176kg)	390lb (177kg)	395lb (179kg)	395lb (179kg)
Fuel capacity	4gal (15.7ltr) or 2gal (9.1ltr)	4gal (18.2ltr) or 2gal (9.1ltr)	4gal (18.2ltr) 2.8 US gal (12.7ltr)	4gal (18.2ltr) 2.8 US gal (12.7ltr)
Oil capacity	4 pints (2.24ltr) (claimed 5 pints)	4 pints (2.24ltr) (claimed 5 pints)	4 pints (2.24ltr)	4 pints (2.24ltr)

LEFT: *The 1976 TR7RV Tiger had a white racing stripe across the top of the UK-model tank. This very original bike has the NVT 'Wiggly Worm' Smiths instruments and the correct labels on the headlamp shell and right-hand switchgear.*

BELOW: *The 1977 Silver Jubilee Bonneville was the Co-op's first limited edition and was a resounding success. This unused example was at the Netley Marsh Eurojumble in September 2008.*

The press really liked the Tiger, citing its lower price, flexibility, economy and easier maintenance as good reasons to buy it over the Bonneville, but the public always preferred the Bonneville; even today a Bonnie commands a price premium over the equivalent Tiger, despite their performance being pretty close. But that is the mystique of the Bonneville name.

A Royal Connection: T140J Jubilee Bonneville

In 1977 the Co-op introduced their first limited edition model, which was produced to celebrate the Silver Jubilee of HRH Queen Elizabeth II. The bike, designated the T140J, was known as the Silver 750 in the UK and the Bonneville Silver Jubilee Limited Edition in the USA. Endorsed by the Royal Family, the bike was the brainchild of Lord Stokes, the ex-chairman of the British Leyland group, who was acting as an unpaid adviser to the Co-op at the time.

Mechanically the bike was the same as the T140V but featured a special silver and blue paint job with red and white pinstriping, chromed outer engine covers, painted wheel-rim centres, a blue seat with red piping, and special badges proclaiming that the bike was a numbered limited edition. Better than standard 'upside-down' Girling gas shocks and top-of-the-range Dunlop K91 'Red Arrow' tyres complemented the unique finish.

The bikes came with a certificate of ownership and initially 1,000 each of the US and UK versions were built. This number was increased

This Jubilee still has the chrome on its brake disks. Note the blue seat, the design of which was used later in the T140E, and the painted and striped front mudguard.

ABOVE: *The Jubilee had special side panels with the Bonneville 750 script and an explanatory panel: the factory eventually produced 2,400 units. Note the red, white and blue pinstriping on the chainguard.*

RIGHT: *The primary chain case, timing cover and gearbox cover were all chrome plated; otherwise the engine was the standard Bonneville unit. The choke lever was always mounted on the carbs on the 750s.*

The timing side of the Jubilee shows the chromed cases. Note the plates on the fuel taps stating their function: US legislation was becoming ever more demanding.

This Jubilee shows a mere 4 miles on the odometer. All the stickers for the warning lights and switches are present and the bike is virtually unused.

With its silver paintwork and patriotic red, white and blue trimmings, the Jubilee was a handsome machine.

by an additional 400 to cater for strong demand from the rest of the Commonwealth. The bikes acquired immediate collector's status and many were salted away by their buyers rather than ridden – an ideal sale for the Co-op as there would be no warranty claims! Overall, though, the bikes were very attractive and many were ridden. The only problem to emerge was the chroming on the aluminium engine cases could corrode and fall off – despite the brochure's

The US model followed the same paint scheme but with the small peanut tank and high bars.

claim that they were:'chrome plated to extremely rigid specifications to add that extra touch of class'.

That aside, the bikes all sold at the time and are still popular more than thirty years later. They come up for sale fairly often, although mint unused examples seem to be getting rare. All in all it was an inspired move by the Co-op: not only did they sell a lot of bikes on the back of the Silver Jubilee, the exercise also helped to raise the profile of Triumph in the UK and the USA.

The Oil-in-Frame Police Bike: TR6P and TR7P Saint

Keeping the Saint moniker, Triumph continued to sell the oil-in-frame single-carburettor 650s and 750s to the police throughout the 1970s. The main difference to the pre-OIF Saint was the widespread adoption of glass–fibre fairings, usually made by Avon Fairings, based in Salisbury, Wiltshire.

The main change from a standard bike was a pair of battery carriers under the seat, one each side of the frame. These were designed to hold two batteries to help supply the ever increasing power demands of police equipment. This in turn meant that the existing side panels were replaced with a much larger glass–fibre moulding to cover the batteries. The bike retained the specially calibrated chronometric speedometer. As the 1970s wore on, demand for the Saint diminished, owing to a combination of competition from the relatively vibration-free Norton Commando-based Interpol, the more comfortable ride offered by BMWs, and the poor (or non-existent) spares situation during the Meriden sit-in.

OPPOSITE TOP: Leading on from the pre-OIF Saint, Triumph produced oil-in-frame models. This is a TR6P with full police kit. Note the reintroduction of the tank-top rack.

OPPOSITE BOTTOM LEFT: The OIF police bikes were built to various specs. This shot shows how much protection the Avon fairing gave to the rider.

OPPOSITE BOTTOM RIGHT: The bikes were equipped with twin 12 volt batteries to power the police equipment. This meant extended side panels, moulded from glass fibre, to cover them.

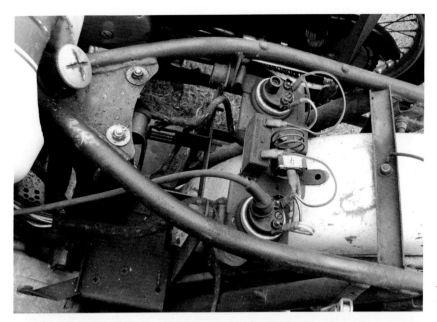

LEFT: *This shot shows the extended battery carriers, allowing for one battery each side of the main frame tube, on the oil-in-frame Saint.*

BELOW: *Triumph continued to pursue the police market to the bitter end. This is the Anti-Vibration Police model, forty-one of which were produced between June 1981 and January 1983.*

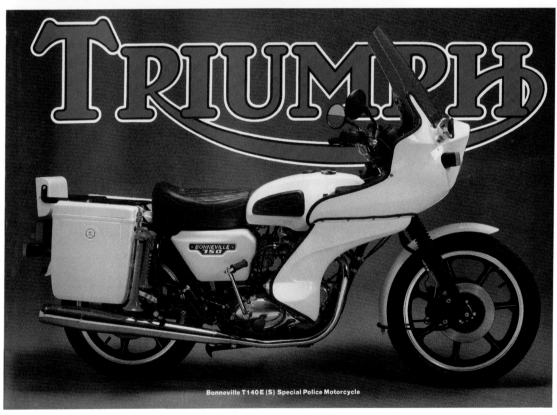

Bonneville T140E (S) Special Police Motorcycle

The UK specification T140E for 1979 kept the 'breadbin' fuel tank from the T140V, but adopted a strangely shaped panel that bore no relationship to the shape of the tank.

Triumph tried to fight back with the Anti-Vibration (AV) model (*see* below), but it was too little, too late, and the Saint name died with the demise of Meriden.

Evolution: T140E and T140ES

Triumph's main market in the 1970s was still the USA, and the increasingly stringent emissions laws proposed by the Environment Protection Agency (EPA) for products sold in the USA meant that the T140V would no longer be allowed to be sold in its existing form.

The new EPA emissions standards were tough. The test regime to measure a vehicle against them meant that a test bike's emissions were measured over 9,500 miles (15,288km), with the results then projected to 19,000 miles (30,576km). The bad news was that the T140V exceeded the allowed level of emissions at 19,000 miles when new, so something had to be done. So before January 1978 Triumph had to

clean up the Bonneville's act. The result was the T140E – with the 'E' standing for 'Emissions'.

While there were numerous changes to the bikes to produce the T140E, three main engineering changes were designed to cut emissions on the new models: a new design of carburettor, electronic ignition and a new cylinder head. The carburettors were Amal Concentric Mk2s, which looked much more modern than the Mk1 but were still a relatively simple design, sharing the Mk1's layout, using a simple cable-operated throttle slide and similar main and pilot jet arrangements. The carburettors' new main casting had squarer lines than the Mk1, and the top was retained by a black plastic screw-on collar, which eased access to the slide and needle.

The carburettors were fitted to the inlet ports using rubber tubes, giving a useful barrier against vibration. Most importantly, the Mk2 Concentric had a 'proper' choke rather than a tickler: one of the EPA's stipulations was that petrol

ABOVE: *The US T140E retained the classic 2 gallon peanut tank. All the 1979 models had the small rack incorporated into the passenger grab rail.*

LEFT: *The T140E lost the famous splayed head, and fitted twin Amal Concentric Mk2 carburettors on parallel inlet ports.*

should not be vented into the atmosphere, something the Mk1 Concentric was particularly good at! So the Mk2 had a proper enriching device that opened an extra jet for cold starts. Both the carburettors' chokes were linked together and were operated by a pressed steel lever mounted on the left-side carburettor. The electronic ignition was Lucas Rita, an optically triggered mechanism with an electronic 'black box' to trigger the sparks and provide an electronic advance/retard. This was a 'fit and forget' item, and meant that the engine would stay in tune without any deterioration of emissions output over the required test mileage: points ignition would drop out of adjustment and have an adverse effect on the emissions during the testing regime. The revised cylinder head had parallel inlet ports with cast-in circular mounts for the carburettors, which meant the bike lost the famous Triumph splayed head look. With some revisions to the combustion chamber shape, this gave improved combustion of the charge, again helping emissions but with a slight loss of power. The compression ratio was dropped from the T140V's 8.25:1 to 7.9:1 to allow the use of four-star fuel, since five star was being phased out. The engine breathing system was set up to breathe into the

air filter, as the EPA stipulated that there should be no emissions from the engine other than those from the exhaust.

Performance was slightly limited by the emissions equipment, but by then the Bonneville was not really seen as an outright sports bike. The modified engine was fitted to bikes supplied to the US market from January 1978 (sometimes called the 1978 ½ model) but this model did not have the cycle part changes detailed below.

In addition to the emissions 'improvements', the Co-op also took the opportunity to introduce a large number of detail improvements to the model for the 'true' 1979 model year, which resulted in a much improved bike. The item that would have an immediate impact on the rider was the new handlebar switchgear, which was still made by Lucas but was based on that used on the Mk3 Norton Commando. It was both better ergonomically and looked a lot more classy, with a black finish and cast-in lettering picked out in white. The switchgear

The TR7RV was not sold in the USA and so did not have the emissions modifications. It did, however, pick up all the other improvements.

incorporated the brake and clutch levers, which were forged alloy and highly polished, and were a major improvement on the chromed steel units formally used. The speedometer and tachometer were mounted in separate rubber and alloy binnacles, and a new instrument panel was positioned between them. This panel had four properly marked warning lights (main beam, indicators, oil pressure and neutral) and a centrally positioned ignition switch, the whole unit being based on the T160 Trident units. Modifications to the gearbox selector were necessary to provide the mechanism to work the neutral light. Moving backwards, there was a proper key-operated lock for the hinged seat and the provision of two small hooks under the seat to store helmets securely. New flat front footrest rubbers with pre-chamfered edges were fitted to replace the round ones used from the 1960s and finally there was a small (15kg maximum load) rear rack integrated with the grab rail. The rear wheel had stronger spokes and the standard fit tyres were now Dunlop K81 TT100s, rather than the T140V's K70s. The frame was powder coated rather than stove enamelled. While this did lead to some problems with the powder coating peeling off some early frames that had not been properly de-greased, ultimately this gave a strong and resilient coating. Negative earth electrics and a new three-phase high output 180 watt alternator completed the picture.

All in all, the T140E was a great improvement on the T140V. The bikes also seemed to be screwed together better (road tests at the time commented on the lack of oil leaks). The improved ancillary items, such as the small rack, better switchgear and the revised three-phase alternator, made the bike an attractive and reliable proposition. Perhaps the most important feature on the bikes was the Lucas Rita electronic ignition. At a stroke this reduced the maintenance requirements and meant that, unless an owner fiddled about with it, the ignition timing could not change either through

wear on the points or the advance retard unit – and I'm sure that the vast majority of problems with Triumph twins can be traced to the ignition system. Meriden also produced a much wider range of colours for the 'E', with four different colour combinations specified for each fuel tank type – US peanut or UK breadbin – and matching colours on the side panels.

While the US-specification peanut tank sported the base colour with contrasting scallops, the paint job on the UK market 4 gallon fuel tank comprised a base metallic colour with a contrasting panel. This panel was an unusual shape, roughly shaped as a parallelogram with a turned-down section at the front and a turned-up section at the rear. While it was distinctive it seemed to be a bit out of place on the bike as its lines didn't follow the styling of the fuel tank at all, and was a far cry from the stylish scallops of the earlier models. As some sort of consolation, Triumph did trumpet the fact that the panel was still lined by hand.

The bikes gained the optional electric starter in March 1980: bikes so equipped were designated the T140ES. In the last full year of Meriden Bonneville production, the T140E and ES could be supplied with the TSS's twin front disc brakes and alloy wheels as optional extras.

Still the Sensible Choice: TR7RV, from 1979

With the introduction of the T140E, with its numerous changes and improvements, the single-carburettor TR7RV was left behind a bit. This was primarily because it was no longer marketed in the USA and so did not get all of the emissions-related kit fitted on the T140E.

The main difference was that the TR7 did not get the new Amal Concentric Mk2 carburettor from 1979: the Tiger was now marketed in the home and general export market as a cost-cutting product, so it had to make do with a 'standard' Mk1 instrument, complete with the tickler – demonstrating that the UK's emission

RIGHT: The instrument panel on the bikes from 1979 was neat and well integrated. Veglia instruments were starting to replace Smiths – but they still could spin round in their rubber binnacles just like on the T140V.

BELOW: This nice T140D Special has a non-standard Norton-style 'peashooter' silencer. Note the rear calliper positioned above the axle, where it was less likely to get covered in road dirt.

legislation was somewhat more lax than that of the USA! The Tiger did benefit, however, from the long list of improvements to the electrics and the cycle parts that the T140E gained, and similarly this resulted in a much better bike.

Factory Customs Meet the Mainstream: T140D Special, 1979–80

By the late 1970s there was a trend for the big four Japanese companies to produce 'Factory Customs' bikes that were firmly based on a production model but with 'chopper' styling cues – nothing too radical but appealing to the 'rebel' market. Triumph realized that it could do the same, and the T140D was the result.

Finished in black, with gold lining on the fuel tank echoing Triumph's traditional scallops, the T140D was the first model to use the cast 'Triumph' script badge on the US-style tank.

The bike was based on the T140E and shared the new head with Mk2 Amal carburettors on parallel inlet ports and Lucas Rita electronic ignition – but the finned cover over the pick-ups was painted black with the edges of the fins picked out in polished alloy.

Inevitably, given the nature of the custom market, the main differences from the mainstream bikes lay in the styling. The wheels were American 'Lester' cast aluminium seven-spoke units: a 19in-diameter front and an 18in rear. While the front tyre was the standard 4.10 × 19 Dunlop TT100 (K81), the rear was a fatter, lower profile 4.25/85 section TT100, which helped to give the chopper look. The seat had a step between the rider and passenger, a new squarer rear grab rail was fitted and the side panels sported two horizontal gold pinstripes below the 'side panel badge', which was the standard shape but boasted a large initial capital on 'Bonneville' in silver above 'Special' in red italics.

The UK-specification T140D Special had the 4-gallon tank, but retained most of the other Special features.

A close-up of the rear end of this UK-specification T140D shows rear calliper, non-standard silencer and the cast alloy wheel.

This brochure shot of the T140D Special shows the stock '2 into 1' exhaust and Lester cast alloy wheels.

The rear mudguard was standard, and the front was a more stylish but less efficient cut-down unit with no rear stay. The exhaust system was a 'two into one', with the twin exhaust pipes sweeping down and under the engine, where they were siamesed and joined a single mega-phone-style silencer on the timing side of the bike. The silencer was terminated with a flat

The TR7T Tiger Trail was aimed at the European 'Big Trailie' niche market.
The off-road style harked back to Triumph's earlier off-road successes.

plate, somewhat reminiscent of the 'black cap' end of a T160/Commando Mark III unit, but finished in chrome. The other main difference to the T140E was the rear brake calliper position; this was carried above the rear axle, out of the mud and grime, and this would become the standard fitting on all Triumphs for 1980.

For 1980 the UK-style 4 gallon fuel tank was an option. While it was still finished in black, the shape of the styling panel on the tank sides, as first seen on the 1978 models, was picked out with gold pinstriping.

The T140D was dropped at the end of the 1980 model year.

A Tiger for the Trail: TR7T/TR6T, from 1981

Even though Meriden was never on a firm financial footing, the Co-op still tried their best to provide what their customers wanted. The TR7T Tiger Trail was just such a product. Instigated by a request from their French distributor, Meriden produced one of the first large trail bikes, which was not quite as outlandish as it seems at first, given Triumph's proud legacy of International Six Days Trials (ISDT) wins. The Tiger Trail was more than just a cosmetic rehash of the road Tiger. It actually showed some real thought in its design, but was ultimately compromised by its road bike ancestry. The changes started at the front, with a 21in wheel and a large plastic motocross-styled mudguard mounted on the lower fork yoke, giving plenty of clearance and the essential trail-bike look.

The small 6in (15.2cm) diameter headlamp had a chromed grill to protect against stones; the high-level braced handlebar was finished in black. No indicators are shown in the brochure, and the instruments came from the poverty-specification Thunderbird, with a speedometer mounted in the left-hand binnacle and the warning lights and ignition switch in the right-hand-side binnacle. A US-specification 2.3 gallon (10.45ltr) fuel tank was used with a three-quarter-length seat. No pillion footrests were shown in the brochure or in the parts lists, but that does not mean they were not fitted, and the rear mudguard was, like the front, a plastic motocross-style item with the rear light carrier built in.

RIGHT: The Tiger Trail had the single-carburettor engine, with a black '2 into 1' exhaust. Folding footrests added to the trail bike feel.

BELOW: The 1981 TR65 Thunderbird was a poverty specification model, designed to fit into a lower insurance group than the 750cc models. Even the brochure that year was in black and white!

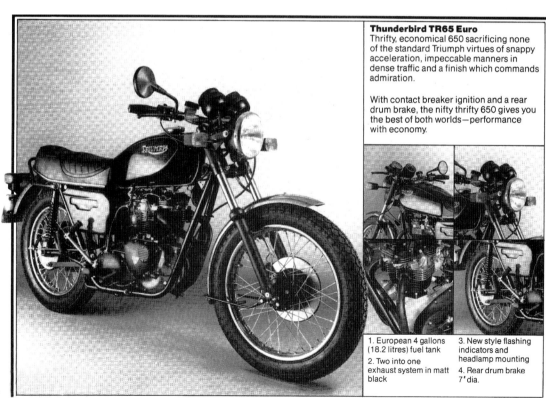

Thunderbird TR65 Euro
Thrifty, economical 650 sacrificing none of the standard Triumph virtues of snappy acceleration, impeccable manners in dense traffic and a finish which commands admiration.

With contact breaker ignition and a rear drum brake, the nifty thrifty 650 gives you the best of both worlds—performance with economy.

1. European 4 gallons (18.2 litres) fuel tank

2. Two into one exhaust system in matt black

3. New style flashing indicators and headlamp mounting

4. Rear drum brake 7" dia.

Tyres were Avon 'Mudplugger' road/trails type knobblies and there was a disc front brake and drum rear. Italian Marzocchi shock absorbers were fitted to take care of the rear suspension. Standard Triumph front forks were fitted, but had black rubber gaiters to protect the stanchions from trail dust and dirt. No centre stand was fitted. The engine was essentially the TR7 Tiger unit, with a single carburettor. The bike had a black 'two into one' exhaust system that swept under the primary chain case and was attached to a large black round-section silencer that followed the line of the frame up to the top of the rear-suspension mount. This was fitted with a wire heat shield. The fuel tank, side panels and mudguards were finished in bright yellow, with a black stick-on decal comprising a stylized 'T' over the 'Triumph' logo on the tank. The bike was certainly striking in appearance and had the macho good looks that big trail bikes seem to need. The bike was only sold in the European market, where it gained a relatively good reception from the press: at the time the trend for big trail bikes was a mainland Europe phenomenon, whereas the British press seemed to be a bit puzzled as to who would buy it.

The 750cc TR7T was only listed for the 1981 model year, and in the 1982 model year was replaced in the official factory lists by the 650cc TR6T. This was broadly similar to the TR7T model, but had an all-black painted 650cc single-carburettor engine and was essentially a TR65 Thunderbird unit. The exhaust system was still siamesed and running under the left-hand side of the engine, but had a new square-section black silencer with a silver stainless steel heat shield, which was pierced with large diameter holes so it almost resembled a BSA B25SS/B50-style silencer; the heat shield was provided as the bike now came with pillion footrests as standard. A black bash plate was fitted under the engine and the headlamp's stone guard had been deleted. The tachometer was reinstated along with the indicators and the central binnacle carrying the warning lights and ignition switch. The brochure also claims a 'modified frame and swinging arm'. The model was available in the previous year's yellow or an even louder bright lime green.

Back to Basics: TR65 Thunderbird

The Thunderbird name was reintroduced into the range with the TR65, which was produced from April 1981, and was available in both UK and US models. While it was based on the then current 750cc models, with their oil-in-frame running gear, the model was introduced as an 'insurance special', as rates for 650cc machines in the UK were cheaper than those for 750cc bikes. The model also had a lower specification than the 750cc bikes, making it cheaper than the Bonneville: in the UK the December 1982 price list shows the TR65 (UK) model price as £1,931, while the T140E Bonneville was £2,086 and the T140E Electric Start Bonneville was £2,137. Oddly, rather than taking the cheap option of sleeving down the 750cc engine bore, Meriden produced a new crank to shorten the stroke of the new model, giving an over-square engine with a bore and stroke of 76 × 71.5mm that was keen to rev.

The cost-cutting measures meant that the bikes were initially introduced without a tachometer and with the ignition/light switch and warning lights housed in the circular tachometer binnacle, while the switch panel between the two clocks was deleted. This one feature shouted 'poverty spec' and made the bike look cheap. Further cost savings were achieved by ditching the electronic ignition and fitting a 120W alternator – there would be no three-phase system here, as was fitted to the other bikes in the range. The bike featured black-painted outer engine cases and fork sliders, a matt black siamesed 'two into one' exhaust system with the silencer on the drive (left) side, and a drum rear brake. Dunlop Gold Seal K70 tyres were specified, again a cost-cutting measure, rather

ABOVE: The TR65 Thunderbird had the '2 into 1' exhaust, giving the timing side a bare look. The engine cases on this model have had the standard black finish polished off.

BELOW: The cost-cutting on the TR65 was most obvious to the rider: no tachometer or instrument binnacle, and the ignition switch and warning lights in the tacho's binnacle.

than fitting the Avon Roadrunners standard to the rest of the range. There was no provision for an electric start as offered on the 750s. The US-styled model (the model was never officially exported to the USA) had the 2.3 gallon peanut fuel tank, while the UK model had the latest rounded version of the 4 gallon tank. Black side panels carried badges with 'Thunderbird' script over Triumph's Thunderbird logo. Despite the obvious cost cutting, the bike was considered to be a quiet and relaxed cruiser that gave very good fuel consumption.

The model did get developed and for 1982 the poverty specification was relaxed, with a tachometer reinstated along with the T140E-style central switch and warning light panel. The black siamesed exhaust system was replaced with a traditional chromed 'two into two' system. The UK model retained its black painted outer engine cases and fork sliders, while the US specification model had these parts polished.

The first TR65 Thunderbird, GDA 30405, was built on 17 June 1981. A total of 213 were built in the 1982 season, and a further 136 were built for the 1983 season.

Touring for the Posh: T140E and T140ES Executive, from 1981

Even as Meriden spiralled down, the Co-op persisted in attacking niche markets and the 1981 model year saw the production of a fully equipped touring version of the Bonneville. Somewhat strangely, however, the Tiger was

The Bonneville Executive was a T140E dressed up with fairing, panniers and top box to provide an 'off the shelf' tourer.

The T140LE in UK specification sported a grey frame, large euro-style fuel tank and low bars.

not used as the basis for this model, presumably because it was no longer on sale in the USA due to emissions issues. The Executive was aimed at the touring market so amply exploited by BMW, and came with a rack, hard panniers, top box and fairing. In fact two types of fairing were available, a small cockpit type, similar to that fitted to the BMW R90S, and a larger model, frame-mounted with detachable lower leg shields to give decent protection to the rider.

The bike looked attractive and by all accounts the luggage and fairings were of a decent quality, but it was not really competitive with the BMW or the specialist Japanese touring models

that were then on the market. The old tech engine counted heavily against it, and performance and comfort were limited by the vertical twin vibes. The bikes could be specified with the electric starter, and in their final year three prototype Anti-Vibration (AV) models were made. In its first year the Executive came in either Smokey Flame or Smokey Blue with gold pinstriping. The following year it came in Smokey Flame or all black, both with gold pinstriping for 1982, and the 1983 Executive AV models were also finished in Smokey Flame and gold pinstriping. The bike was a sterling effort that produced a good machine, but it was really too little, too late.

More Royal Connections: T140LE 'Royal Wedding', 1981

The wedding of Charles, Prince of Wales, and Lady Diana Spencer on 29 July 1981 gave Triumph a marketing opportunity to produce another limited edition version of the Bonneville, just as they did with the 1977 Jubilee Bonneville. The T140LE was released in July 1981, and its design followed the same formula as the Jubilee, being a basically standard Bonneville with a special finish, unique to the variant. The bike came in three variants: two home market bikes, one based on the UK style and the second based on the US style, and the variant that was actually exported to the USA.

The UK style variant had a painted silver frame, and all-black engine, Morris seven-spoke alloy wheels in black with silver highlights, and a black seat. The fuel tank was chromed. This was the first time chrome had been used on a production model Triumph's tank since the 1950s, and the tank's cast 'Triumph' logo had slim black-painted scallops lined in gold above and below it. The side panels were black: gloss uppers and matt lowers, with the join between the matt and gloss paint delineated with a gold pinstripe. The side panels carried the standard-

The T140LE Royal in US specification had a two-tone seat and chromed 2 gallon peanut tank. The model was fitted with a single front disc.

shaped badge, with gold 'BONNEVILLE Royal' lettering and a small stylized version of the Prince of Wales's feathers heraldic emblem on a black background. A small 'LIMITED EDITION' logo in plain capitals adorned the lower rear of the side panel. Polished stainless steel mudguards gave some glitter, black indicator bodies, headlamp body and mounting ears and black fork sliders were featured, and twin front discs finished off the bike in style. This made for a striking and attractive design that was just the right side of tasteful.

The second home-market model was based on the US-styled Bonneville and was a bit less restrained. While it did have a black-painted frame, it featured a polished engine, chromed spoked wheels and a chromed US-style peanut fuel tank. This had chromed 'picture frame' Triumph badges with a blue and gold-lined scallop running over and under the badge. The bike had high US-style bars and a single front disc. The side panels were in blue, with the front and lower edges darkening almost to black, with a gold pinstripe. As before the side panel had a gold 'LIMITED EDITION' logo on its lower half and a 'BONNEVILLE Royal' badge, but this time with black lettering on a silver background. The seat was a 'King and Queen'-style unit, with black sides and grey seating areas, and looked truly garish. The fork sliders and the bottoms of the instrument binnacles were polished alloy; mudguards were polished stainless steel and the

The US-market specific T140LE Royal was the most restrained of the three types. Only fifty of this version were made.

headlamp mounting ears and indicator bodies were all in chrome, although all those the author has seen in person had black indicator bodies.

The third variant was exported to the USA, but was based on the European model. David Gaylin, in his *Triumph Motorcycle Restoration Guide: Bonneville and TR6, 1956–1983*, identifies that a maximum of fifty of this variant were built since the US market had cooled towards the Royal Family by then. Documented alongside the 'standard' Bonneville and the Bonneville Executive, the Royal was basically the UK variant described above, but with frame, side panels and fuel tank all in black, with gold pinstriping on the tank and side panels. The top half of the engine was also black, and the crankcases were polished alloy. The styling of this version was less radical than the other two models, and was a very attractive model in its own right.

Triumph produced only 250 of the T140LE models. These provided an attractive alternative to the mainstream bikes in the range. The US bike was featured in the three-model US brochure for 1982, while the two home-market models were publicized in a dedicated four-page brochure. All in all, they were a worthy attempt to capitalize on the Royal Wedding fever that spread over the UK at the time, but did not prove to be as popular as the Jubilee model.

Last Gasp: TSX Factory Custom

The TSX, introduced in June 1982, was a 'factory custom' bike that gave a nod to the 'cruiser' culture that was starting to emerge at that time. Triumph described the styling of the bikes as the 'low-slung "West Coast" look', and the bike was a more radical successor to the T140D Special.

The TSX style was based on the US 'West Coast' look. Still based on the T140, the bike succeeded in its aim of looking good.

The 8-valve TSS was the ultimate development of the Meriden twin. With up-to-date running gear, it was a real contender.

The bike was a subtly restyled T140, retaining the T140ES's 2-valve, electric start engine, but having revised seat, tank and side panels. The TSX used cast alloy wheels made by Morris, with a narrow 19in-diameter front and a fat 16in on the rear. Tyres were a wide section 5.10 × 16 at the rear and a skinny 3.25 × 19 on the front, giving the essential custom look. Italian-made Paioli rear shock absorbers were used, and were relocated some 2in (5cm) rearwards, with revised brackets on the rear sub-frame, and the bottom mounts on the swinging arm positioned above the wheel axle. The rear disc brake was operated by a Brembo rear brake master cylinder, reflecting the equipment used on the Les Harris Bonneville later in the decade, while the callipers were still Lockheed items. The 7in (17.8cm) diameter headlamp was mounted on a new bracket made of chromed wire, which, while looking back to the 1971 bikes, was much more substantial.

The front Lucas indicators were also relocated to the bottom yoke, with the chrome steel tubes mounted behind the fork stanchions. The late-style instrument binnacle, as first seen on the T160 Trident, was used, housing the speedometer and tachometer with the idiot lights and ignition switch mounted between them. A new chrome cover was fitted between the top and bottom yokes, covering the top of the stanchions. The engine was standard Bonneville, but the twin carburettors were German-made 32mm CV Bing units and were exposed by the truncated side panels, unlike the other models fitted with these carburettors. The rear of the new restyled rounded fuel tank was integrated into the front of the new dual seat, giving a smooth line to the bike. The seat had a raised back section and, while not quite a classic 'King and Queen' item, did have a certain custom style. The exhaust system featured short megaphone-styled silencers with vertically slash-cut ends, and also featured a balance pipe repositioned under the engine, rather than close to the head as on the standard models.

Colours for the fuel tank, mudguard and side panels were either Black or Burgundy Red, with black frame and polished alloy fork sliders and outer engine cases. The engine's crankcases, barrel and head were black, with polished fin edges on the head and rocker boxes. In a break with tradition, the TSX was the first Triumph to have vinyl decals, in the shape of red, orange and yellow swept-back decals on the fuel tank and side panels rather than contrasting colours separated by hand-crafted pinstriping. The TSX was a good-looking bike. By all accounts it handled well and was pleasant to ride, although apparently it was less steady at high speed due to the mix of wheel sizes. Development of the bike was proposed, and for the 1983 model year Triumph were looking to install the 8-valve TSS engine in it to produce the TSX8, but this development was overtaken by events and the bike was never produced. Triumph produced 381 of the TSX model: the first one (CMO31861) was built on 27 October 1981 and the last (KEA 34353) on 21 December 1982.

Note that the 'CMO' numbering system falls outside of the standard Triumph numbering system, and was used at the time to disguise the manufacturing date to avoid paying an increased motorcycle tax based on the date of the bike's manufacture.

Performance Returned: TSS 8-Valve

The TSS model was introduced in 1982 and represented the first major change to the Triumph twin motor produced by Meriden. The aim of the model was to re-establish Triumph as a performance-oriented marque, and the model was marketed as one of the fastest 750cc production motorcycles in the world.

The TSS produced a claimed 57bhp at 6,500rpm, while a 1975 T140V produced 52bhp at 6,200rpm and a 1981 T140D Bonneville produced a lowly 49.5bhp at 6,500rpm (figures quoted from *Bike* magazine). The performance of the TSS was a great improvement over the 2-valve Bonneville. In the UK, *Bike* magazine achieved a one-way best of 122.24mph (196.72km/h) out of their test bike in August 1982, which was just faster than the 1977 Suzuki GS750 (121.95mph/196.25km/h) they tested in March 1977 and the Honda CB750 tested in March 1981 (119.6mph/192.47km/h). So Triumph's claim in its literature that the TSS was 'one of the fastest 750cc production motorcycles in the world' was not as outlandish as first it seems! *Bike* magazine also reckoned the TSS was a good 20mph faster than the T140Ds they had tested and about 10mph faster than the 'standard' 2-valve Bonneville, demonstrating that the TSS's performance was a substantial improvement over the 2-valve bikes – especially the later ones that had been strangled by the US emission requirements.

The engine was the heart of the TSS. While retaining the layout of the previous 750cc engine, it featured a beefed-up bottom end and a completely new barrel and head. The engine's top end had four valves per cylinder, operated by pushrods and forked rocker arms to improve breathing, and therefore produced more power at higher revs. The bottom end featured narrower, but larger diameter, big-end journals, making a strong and stiff crank that was able to handle the increased power of the TSS motor.

With its 32mm Mk2 Amal Concentric carburettors, compression ratio of 9.5:1 and modern efficient combustion chamber, the TSS could run happily on four-star fuel (95 Octane) and still return a decent fuel consumption of around 45mpg (6.3ltr/100km). The engine's top end, barrel and crankcases were finished in an attractive silky heat-reflective black finish, while the primary chain case, timing cover and gearbox cover were finished in natural polished aluminium.

The TSS's 8-valve top end was a development of the 1960s Weslake unit. The engine also featured a beefed-up bottom end.

The TSS running gear had one major change to that of the standard T140, as it had twin 9.8in (250mm) diameter front discs, which were much needed given the increase in performance! The rest of the bike's running gear was essentially to the same specification as the Bonneville. The 4-gallon fuel tank and side panels were finished in black with gold pinstriping and alloy wheels (seven-spoke Morris type) were offered as an optional extra. Data from Roy Shilling of the Triumph Owners' Motor Cycle Club (TOMCC) indicates that 438 T140W (TSS) models were produced, starting with cmO32063, built on 27 October 1981, and culminating with BEA 34392, built on 6 January 1983.

Post-Meriden: Les Harris 'Devon' Bikes

With the termination of production at Meriden in January 1983, and the subsequent sale of the company assets and the site to John Bloor, things looked bleak for the Turner-designed twins. However, in order to keep the Triumph name alive until the new Bloor Triumphs were ready for production, John Bloor licensed Les Harris,

BELOW: The TSS's eight valves promoted better breathing, higher revs and more power. The TSS motor produced a claimed 57bhp at 6,500rpm, while a T140V produced a claimed 52bhp at 6,200rpm.

ABOVE: Twin discs were fitted as standard to the TSS to cater for the increased performance.

LEFT: The Les Harris bikes were made in UK or US styles, but were not officially imported into the USA. The UK version had the larger fuel tank.

an established Triumph spares manufacturer, to build the Bonneville and Tiger models from a new UK factory in Newton Abbot, Devon. The licence was limited and allowed the manufacture of the Bonneville in only UK or US specification. The specification was limited to that of the last T140, so developments first seen on the TSS, such as the alloy barrel and stronger crank, could not be included.

While some of the tooling was recovered from the factory, many of the jigs and other tooling were either lost or unusable, resulting in much unexpected work being needed to get the bikes back into production. Many of the original suppliers to Meriden were no longer involved in the production of motorcycle parts, so the Devon operation had to cast their net wide to find replacements. These included sourcing the front fork legs and sliders from Paioli, but using Triumph yokes and using rear shocks from the same company. The Brembo brake callipers also came from Italy, as did the Lafranconi silencers. Switchgear was supplied by Magura of Germany, as was the front-brake master cylinder, and Veglia supplied the speedometer and tachometer. The mudguards were of polished stainless steel.

The engine was constructed to the final T140 specification, but had a modified crank with TSS-type flywheel, though with standard big-end and main-bearing sizes. The crankcases were cast from the original Meriden dies, but benefited from much more accurate machining from the Harris organization's new machine tools. While the cylinder barrel was supposed to be cast iron, some of the bikes 'escaped' from the factory with alloy barrels, with the consequential advantages of better cooling and lower weight. The alloy barrel was available as an aftermarket kit, costing around £300. All barrels on the bikes, cast iron or alloy, were initially painted silver for 1985, but reverted to black paint in 1986. The cylinder head carried twin Mark 1½ Amal Concentric carburettors, which were basically the Mk1 design with the Mk2 cold-start mechanism replacing the Mk1's ticklers,

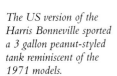
The US version of the Harris Bonneville sported a 3 gallon peanut-styled tank reminiscent of the 1971 models.

The Harris Bonneville is still popular and owners continue to run and modify them. Here is Darrell Babkirk's 1987 model. Note the Brembo rear disc and the master cylinder positioned outside of the frame tubes giving better access and protection from road dirt.

and the air filter boxes were modified to make a better fit to the frame and carburettors than the Meriden-built units.

The bikes were introduced to the UK market in June 1985. They were well received and quickly gained a reputation for reasonable quality, quiet running and good performance. Their performance was a slight improvement on the T140E and the engine was considered to be smoother by contemporary road testers. The downside was the somewhat random quality of the Italian suspension components and the use of poor quality chrome, which led to premature rusting of some wheel rims and other ancillaries. Production was finally stopped in March 1988. One explanation for the ending of production was that the dies used to produce the crankcases needed replacing, and the cost was prohibitive. Approximately 1,257 were produced over the three years of production (engine frame numbers from 000003 to 001258). The bike was succeeded by the Rotax 500cc single-powered Matchless G80 – but that is another story. Unfortunately, despite a strong demand, the bikes were never formally exported to the USA since the product insurance and emission testing required was too expensive.

4 The Swansong Models for 1983

With its finances in an increasingly perilous state, the Co-op factory continued to plan for new models even as the axe fell. The factory produced brochures for a range of bikes for 1983, all variants on the existing bikes but still exhibiting some fresh thinking and a wider range of models than before. The full Triumph range proposed for 1983 comprised eight models:

- Bonneville UK
- Bonneville USA
- TSS
- TSX4
- TSX8
- Daytona 600
- Thunderbird 600
- Special Police Motorcycle.

This wide range reflects Meriden's switch from a concern aimed at the mass market into a low-volume producer aiming at niche markets. All of the proposed bikes had electric start as standard. The range can be split into two types of bike: road sports-oriented machines, which were conventionally styled, and machines with the West Coast 'low rider' look pioneered by the previous year's TSX model.

The proposed road sports-oriented models were the Bonneville UK, TSS and Daytona 600. These bikes featured what Triumph called 'lean machine' styling, the most important feature being rear-set footrests and low handlebars to give a sports-oriented riding position to address the perennial gripe of riders and journalists, since the introduction of the left-foot gear change range, that the footrests were

The proposed 1983/84 UK-specification Bonneville was closely based on the previous year's model. The rear-set footrests were the main alteration.

Like the 1983/84 Bonneville, the 1983/84 TSS was largely unchanged, apart from paint colours and rear-set footrests. It was, however, fitted with the AV frame previously seen on the Police bikes.

too far forward for fast riding. The change of riding position was achieved by designing a new linkage for the gear pedal that was mounted on the primary chain case, and shorter footrest hangers and a revised brake pedal, effectively moving the rider's feet back 3 or 4 inches (7.6–10cm). This linkage had first been revealed in December 1976, when *Bike* magazine ran an article on the Meriden Co-op that featured a shot of the 'Premium Bonneville', the experimental shop's idea of developments to the Bonnie. This included the rear-set footrests and the seat and rear cowling seen on the 1983 machines, and also had T140E-style instruments, three-spoke alloy wheels, T160 Trident-type silencers and Amal Mk2 carburettors.

All three road sports bikes used the Italian-made 4 gallon fuel tanks, with die-cast 'Triumph' badges, a restyled chunky seat with new flat 'U'-shaped rear passenger grab rail and a small fairing behind the seat that reached almost to the rear light. Stainless steel mudguards were fitted. The Bonneville UK and Daytona 600 had a single 9.8in (250mm) disc brake with Lockheed calliper and a rear drum brake, which to quote the brochure was introduced 'following many rider requests' – so not a cost-cutting measure! Both models used the original two valves per

cylinder, the Bonneville UK retaining its 750cc capacity, while the Daytona 600 had a short-stroke 600cc motor to keep it in a lower UK insurance bracket. The Daytona also featured 30mm Amal Mk1½ carburettors, while the Bonneville UK had the 30mm Amal Mk2.

The TSS had the 4-valve per cylinder 750cc motor, with twin Amal concentric Mk2 carburettors, and retained the previous year's twin discs up front, and a single disc on the rear. It also had the Anti-Vibration frame with its rubber mounting for the engine (*see* Chapter 5), and featured handsome seven-spoke alloy wheels.

The custom-styled Bonneville USA and Thunderbird 600 featured a single front disc and drum rear brake, high bars, thick dual-level seat and painted mudguards. A 16in spoked rear wheel carried a fat tyre to give the West Coast low rider look, a 19in spoked front gave a lean look and the small 2.8 gallon fuel tank featured vinyl stick-on graphics as on the 1982 TSX. Both custom models had short slash-cut silencers, and the balance pipe was repositioned under the engine.

The 750cc Bonneville USA retained the Bonneville's trademark twin 30mm carburettors, Bing CV types being fitted, but was styled like

ABOVE: *A new insurance-beating model was the sporting 600cc Daytona. With the stroke shortened to 66mm from the 750cc models' 82mm, the engine was very undersquare, so it should have revved like a good un!*

RIGHT: *The 1983/84 750cc US-specification Bonneville was closely styled on the TSX, with a big back wheel and drum rear brake. The low-slung styling was described as 'West Coast' by Triumph.*

OPPOSITE TOP: *Very similar in style to the US Bonneville, the 600cc Thunderbird shared its short-stroke engine with the 600cc Daytona.*

OPPOSITE BOTTOM: *It's hard to see where the TSX 4 Valve fits into the model range as the styling is very close to the US Bonneville and Thunderbird. The alloy wheels and rear disc brake give it a better specification than the Bonnie and T'bird.*

the TSX, with spoked wheels, a fat 16in rear and slim 19in front. The bike featured the 2-valve per cylinder, electric-start engine, with the Bonneville having a slightly higher tuned motor than the TSX4 with a 7.9:1 compression ratio.

The Thunderbird 600 was also based on the TSX factory custom seen in 1982, but its electric-start engine was further de-stroked from the previous years 650cc, with a bore and stroke of 76 × 66mm giving a capacity of 599cc. The Thunderbird's engine was in the same state of tune as the Daytona 600 with a compression ration of 8.4:1, but had only one 30mm Amal Mk1½ carburettor.

The other custom-styled bikes were the TSX4 and TSX8. These differed from each other in the frame and engine, with the TSX4 having the standard frame and the same 2-valve engine as the Bonneville USA (but with a 7.4:1 compression ration), while the TSX8 had the Anti-Vibration frame and the TSS 4-valve per cylinder motor, but also, rather worryingly, the same brakes as the TSX4, with single front

The TSX8 was a bit of a worry! The TSS motor popped into a West Coast custom bike must have made an interesting combination. While research indicates that Triumph was proposing to use the AV frame for the TSX8, the brochure and the specification shows a standard frame.

and rear discs. Both the TSX4 and the TSX8 had twin 32mm CV carburettors, and seven-spoke alloy rims, a wide 16in diameter on the rear and a skinny 19in on the front. These models looked very similar to the Thunderbird and Bonneville USA, and it is hard to see why Meriden was intending to produce such similar models – unless the TSXs were for the USA market, and the Thunderbird and Bonneville USA were aimed at the UK market.

The final bike in the proposed range was the 'Special Police Motorcycle'. This bike was an attempt to resurrect the 'Saint' and was aimed at the police and other 'fleet' user markets. The bike's main feature was the use of the Anti-Vibration frame, named the 'Enforcer', which was fitted to enable the bike to compete with the smooth German and Japanese opposition in the fleet market. The bike featured a single seat, large fairing and Craven panniers mounted on a carrier that incorporated a rubber-mounted radio platform and an illuminated rear 'Police Stop'

sign. The bike was available with either of the 750cc motors, the Bonneville or TSS, and in the brochure is shown with TSS-style twin-disc front brakes and seven-spoke cast alloy wheels.

Finally, rumour has it that Meriden was bravely following the Japanese lead by apparently deleting the kick-starter on the bikes. I had not been able to get a definitive answer to this question by the time this book went to press, but none of the brochure shots I've seen show a kick-starter fitted to the proposed 1983 bikes, and there is a smart bung filling the hole in the gearbox cover where the kick-start lever was supposed to go.

While these models did have significant improvements made when compared to the previous year's models, they were relatively minor modifications to an ageing range, when what Meriden really needed in order to survive was a new model range. Time had run out for the Co-op by February 1983 and the plant was closed before these models could see the light of day.

The 1983/84 model year Police model, equipped with a new fairing and AV frame, makes for a futuristic looking bike. The bike came with the option of 4- or 8-valve 750cc motors.

5 Anti-Vibration: The Final Hope

Anyone who has ridden a Triumph twin will know that parallel twins do vibrate – the main issue between various models is how much! Taking the causes of 360-degree twins' vibration at a simplistic level, the main vibration of a 360-degree parallel twin is in the vertical plane – the engine tries to go 'up and down' – with some much less intrusive 'side to side' vibrations as a result of the firing impulses. In the 1970s Triumph lost most of its police business to Norton and BMW, mainly due to the unacceptable levels of vibration. As the 1980s dawned, Triumph wanted to get back into the police market, especially as Norton was no more. In the mid-1970s GKN carried out some work on the Triumph 750cc twin engine and produced a prototype engine, designated T140MF, with a balance mechanism that cut down vibration considerably. However, this pure engineering approach was not pursued, and when Triumph revisited the issue they perceived the way ahead was to rubber mount the engine.

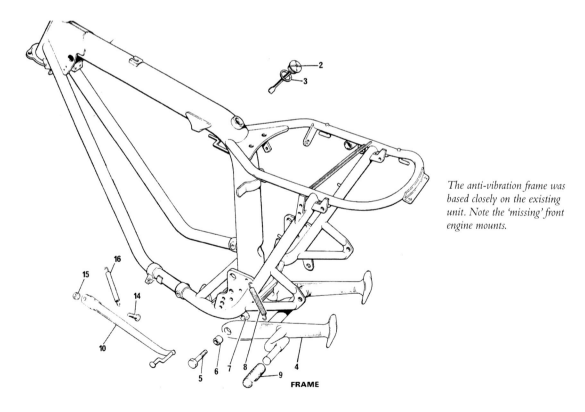

The anti-vibration frame was based closely on the existing unit. Note the 'missing' front engine mounts.

95

While rubber mounting of car engines was commonplace, the only mainstream British bikes of the post-war period to feature anti-vibration mounts for the engine were the BSA-built Sunbeam S7 and S8 models and the Norton Commando. The Sunbeam S7 was introduced in 1947 and was produced along with the S8 until 1956. The Sunbeam was a 500cc parallel twin mounted longitudinally and had rubber mounting introduced very late in its development cycle (or early in the production cycle, depending on how you look at it) when the vibration levels of the pre-production versions of the twin were found to be unacceptable.

The rubber mounting was achieved using rubber block-type engine mounts on the front and rear of the engine and gearbox. These were very car-like, being bolted together with a car-type single-plate clutch housed in a bell housing between the engine and gearbox. With the final drive being by shaft, a Layrub universal joint connected the gearbox output to the drive shaft, and with its built-in rubber bushing it could handle both the engine and gearbox unit's movement and the rear suspension movement. Technically the overall package was successful, managing to isolate much of the engine vibration from the rider, but the Sunbeam was never that successful commercially as it was aimed at the somewhat limited 'Gentleman's Tourer' market.

The second successful British bike that used rubber mounting was the Norton Commando, with its unique 'Isolastic' (Isolation Elastic) rubber mounting system. The Norton, initially a 750cc parallel twin and later enlarged to 828cc, took the concept of rubber mounting a step further than the Sunbeam. With its chain drive and 'conventional' engine gearbox configuration, just rubber mounting the engine and gearbox would result in problems with the chain rear drive: if the engine and gearbox were moving, the chain tension would be badly affected and the chain alignment could lead to the chain jumping off the sprockets. By isolating

The bottom engine mount used rubber blocks on each side, joined by a 'bridge' piece to connect the engine to the frame. The engine had limited movement up, down and sideways.

the complete engine, gearbox and swing arm from the frame, forks and footrests, Norton overcame the driveline problems, which did not occur with the Sunbeam as it had shaft drive.

In the Norton solution, special tubular steel mounts with round rubber inserts were used front and rear, which allowed the engine and gearbox to move in the vertical plane, but used shims (and later adjustable 'vernier' adjusters) to control the side-to-side movement of the complete engine, gearbox and swinging arm unit. The whole system was very successful in both cutting down vibration and preserving the Norton reputation for handling and roadholding. It also helped to preserve the various ancillary components on the bike that were susceptible to vibration, such as instruments and electrics, and the comfort afforded to the rider was a major factor in many UK police forces changing from Saints to Norton Interpols (Commando-based police models). However, the Norton system did have some downfalls. The first system used shims to set up the correct amount of side play: too little clearance would transmit vibration through to the rider, too much and handling was affected.

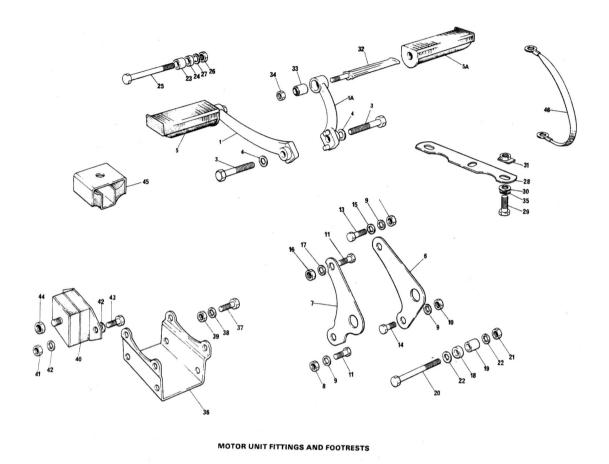

MOTOR UNIT FITTINGS AND FOOTRESTS

The lower rubber engine mounts and their 'bridge' piece formed the mainstay of the AV system.

Adjustment was fiddly and required the correct-sized shims to be fitted. The last system, fitted to the Mark 3 Commando, featured a screw-operated vernier adjustment mechanism that eased the maintenance burden somewhat, but still needed precise adjustment. The system was covered by a number of patents, and when the Co-op started looking at anti-vibration (AV) systems they had to find a system that did not infringe the patents held by their former owners, NVT. Help came in the form of Bernard Hooper, formerly Norton's head development engineer, who had left Norton in 1975 and set up Bernard Hooper Engineering Ltd, where he designed 'System 360', an anti-vibration system for motorcycles that did not infringe any patents and would be, as far as was possible, maintenance-free. The system used rubber blocks, rather than Norton's tubular mounts, and mounted the engine at three points: at the cylinder head, under the crankcases, and at the back of the gearbox. The head and crankcase mounts used bonded rubber mouldings and pressed steel mounts to isolate the engine from the frame. The rear mount had to preserve the chain line and tension, and comprised two new engine plates that bolted directly onto the back of the engine unit at the gearbox and primary chain case. These plates carried the swinging arm pivot, so the swinging arm was attached rigidly to the engine unit. A second spindle was positioned below the swinging arm spindle and was attached to each end of the swing arm spindle using vertical arms. This arrangement allowed the swing arm to move in a controlled manner in an arc around the lower pivot, giving slight fore and aft movement – enough to take up the movement allowed by two rubber mounts – and was intended to keep the chain tension and alignment within acceptable limits, while still allowing full suspension travel. Anecdotal evidence, however, shows that this aim was not necessarily met, with the owner

of one machine having to install a trials-type chain tensioner to stop the chain jumping off the sprockets. So the whole engine and swinging arm was able to rock up and down independently of the frame while pivoting on the secondary rear spindle. This meant that the vibration in the up and down plane (the plane in which the Triumph's engine vibrated the most) could be accommodated by the rubber mounts while the swinging arm pivot (and the whole rear of the engine unit) could not move from side to side, hence preserving wheel alignment and hence handling. Incidentally, the front engine-mounting lugs were removed from the frame and a new crosspiece was inserted below their position to brace the twin down tubes – an easy recognition point. This gave

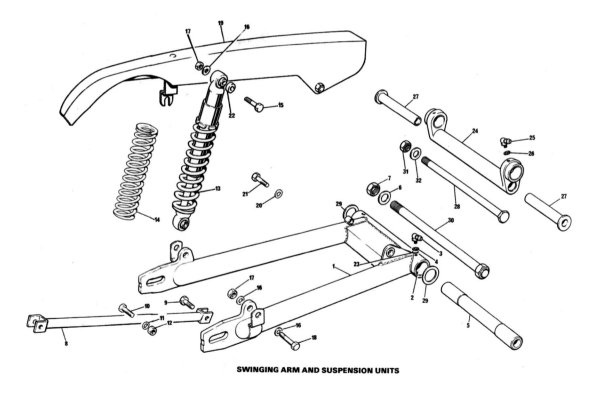

SWINGING ARM AND SUSPENSION UNITS

The AV swinging-arm fixing allowed the engine to move in the vertical plane while keeping the swinging arm fixed in relation to the engine to maintain a correct chain line.

Summary of Anti-Vibration Frame Bikes Build			
Frame number	*Build dates*	*Model*	*Number*
GDA 30404	16 June 1981	T140AV	1
HAD 31211–31219	13 & 14 July 1981	T140AV	9
NDA 31901–31912	20 & 21 Oct 1981	T140E/S AV	12
NDA 31913–31917	21 Oct 1981	TR7 AV	5
NDA 31918	29 Oct 1981	T140 AV	1
BDA 31924	4 Dec 1981	T140 AV	1
BEA 33007–33008	15 Feb 1982	T140AV	2
GEA 33526–33527	10 June 1982	T140E/S AV Exec	2
KEA 34067	10 Sept 1982	T140E/S AV Exec	1
KEA 34127–34128	29 Sept 1982	T140W AV (TSS)	2
KEA 34212–34213	11 Oct 1982	T140E/S AV	2
KEA 34229	3 Nov 1982	T140 AV Twin Alternator	1
KEA 34324	Frame only	T140W AV (TSS)	1
BEA 34392	6 Jan 1983	T140W AV (TSS)	1

Data provided by Roy Shilling of the Triumph Owners' Motorcycle Club (TOMCC)

Triumph a system that could, with a bit more development to address the chain tension issues, have resulted in a bike that was acceptable to the police and other fleet users of motorcycles. The motors used in the AV frame had their balance factor changed to 55 per cent to ensure smooth running.

Experiments at the factory using accelerometers to measure vibration at the footrests, handlebars and seat showed an overall reduction of approximately 60 per cent between a standard bike and an AV-framed example. This was a significant reduction and gave a major improvement to rider comfort, especially at higher speeds. The AV frames were codenamed 'Enforcer', another pointer to the police market the bike was aimed at.

The factory plan was to introduce the AV frame in the 1983 season. It was first going to be used on the 8- and 4-valve Police models, and on the 8-valve 'civilian' models, the TSS and TSX8. The 1983 brochures show these bikes with the AV frame. Before the system could be put into production, however, Meriden stopped

production and closed having made a total of forty-three AV models. These were produced between June 1981 and January 1983.

A twin-alternator model made in 1982 was an experimental bike for the potential police customers. It housed two Lucas alternators side by side, with an extended crank and primary chain case to accommodate the extra rotor and stator. The intention was to double the electrical power available to power the ever increasing levels of equipment needed to meet the requirements of the 1980s police forces. However, the 1983 range never saw the light of day, so the project died with the Meriden factory. (Unfortunately, Les Harris was not allowed to use the AV frame under the terms of his licence with the new Triumph Company.)

The system lives on, however, as Hooper sold the production rights to Harley-Davidson, after demonstrating the system on a FLT model. Hooper still had Triumph's interests in mind, however, since the rights sold to Harley-Davidson included a clause to allow Triumph to continue to produce the system.

6 Competition History

When the 650cc unit twin was introduced in 1963, Triumph was not formally involved in racing, largely owing to a policy adopted by Edward Turner, who saw racing as a diversion away from building and selling bikes rather than as a marketing ploy to help with the bike sales. While this was the situation in the UK, Triumph was being successful in events in the USA, where the 'race on Sunday, sell on Monday' philosophy of many dealers led to sponsorship of riders in off-road events, such as the big 'hare and hounds' desert races, flat-track and oval racing. To meet the demand the factory started producing competition versions of the Bonneville and TR6, and there was a thriving aftermarket in off-road frames and running gear. The factory

The US-only TT Bonneville came with no lights or silencers. This 1966/67 model was spotted at Netley Marsh autojumble in September 2008, having been freshly reimported back from the USA.

took this support further with the highly tuned Bonneville TT Specials of the mid-1960s, which led to many Triumph wins in TT racing. The tacit official support given to Triumph riders in the USA culminated in the T120RT, the 750cc Bonneville put together by the US distributor.

In the USA there were three types of racing relevant to the big unit Triumph: California desert racing, Class C and TT racing. For the California desert racing, as epitomized by the 'Big Bear' event, Triumph was in decline by 1963 when the big unit twins were introduced since the small-capacity two strokes were already taking over. The Class C dirt track and road race category was limited to 500cc overhead valve (ohv) machines until a ruling by the American Motorcycle Association (AMA) allowed ohv machines up to 750cc to compete in the series from 1969.

This opened up the field to the 650cc Triumphs (and for 1970 the 750cc T120RTs) and resulted in a number of wins in 1969. For 1970 the 750cc T120RTs dominated the class and continued to do so for 1971. In contrast Triumph dominated the TT class from 1963, with their 650cc Bonnevilles winning time after time. For example, in the 1964 Ascot 50 Mile National, Triumphs scooped the first seven places, and Triumphs won it again in 1965. The T120 TT special played a major part in these wins and the 650cc Triumph-engined machines kept winning into the early 1970s, albeit in modified form and often with specialist frames from makers such as the appropriately named Trackmaster.

At home in the UK in the early 1960s motor cycle sport was either the Grand Prix-type racing or moto-cross, both dominated by exotic works machinery such as the BSA B44 Victor. However, racing based on production machines was being held in the UK at the time, and one of the more famous races was the 500-mile endurance race at Thruxton in Hampshire, first run in 1955. Triumph had built up an impressive number of victories in the event by 1963. The first appearance of the new unit 650 models came at the 1964 event, when Percy Tait piloted a unit 650 Bonneville into second place. In 1965, by when the event had moved to the Castle Combe circuit as the condition of the Thruxton track had deteriorated and was considered too dangerous for racing, the race was won by a 650 Bonneville ridden by Dave Degans and Barry Lawton. In the same year Triumph introduced the 'Thruxton Bonneville' as an 'off the shelf' production racer, based on the experience gained in the 500-mile event (*see* Chapter 2). The event moved to Brands Hatch in 1966, where Triumph Bonnevilles dominated the winner enclosure until 1968, before returning to a restored Thruxton for 1969. This was the Thruxton Bonnevilles' swansong, as they claimed the first three places, with Percy Tait and Malcolm Uphill taking first place. For 1970,

Percy Tait and Malcolm Uphill won the 1969 Thruxton 500-mile race on a T120 Thruxton Bonneville.

The Thruxton was a potent production racer. Few were made and they are desirable today. With their production-racing ancestry, they make true roadburners.

Triumph's production racing efforts were switched to the 750cc Trident, leaving the Thruxton Bonneville as an iconic race-winning machine.

With the introduction of a production class race for 250cc, 500cc and 750cc bikes at the Isle of Man TT for 1967, Triumph's successes at Thruxton meant that they could return to the Isle of Man TT races with a good chance of winning. This was a three-lap race over the arduous mountain circuit of 37¼ miles (60km) per lap, and win they did – in the 1967 event John Hartle won the 750cc class on a factory-prepared Thruxton Bonneville with a best recorded speed of 130.4mph (209.8km/h), and a fastest lap of 97.87mph (157.5km/h). The following year, 1968, Triumph entered three Thuxtons: both John Hartle and Rod Gould crashed, but Malcolm Uphill finished fifth, with a race average of 88.08mph (141.75km/h). The winner, Ray Pickrell riding a Dunstall (Norton) Dominator, averaged 99.39 mph (159.95km/h). The first 100mph lap for the production class was within reach. Uphill was again entered by Triumph for 1969 on a Thruxton. This bike, registration number MAC 232E, was very carefully

prepared by the Triumph race shop staff. It was surprisingly stock, with just high-compression pistons and Spitfire-form cams, along with the Thruxton 'ciger'-type straight-through silencers, Amal Concentric carburettors and rerouted exhaust pipes. Running gear was close to stock, with the standard TLS front brake, but an alloy fuel tank, racing seat and alloy rims helped to cut down some weight and the dolphin fairing helped with top speed. Uphill ran a Dunlop K81 rear tyre and a triangular racing tyre on the front. In his first lap, covered from a standing start, Uphill averaged 100.09mph (161.07km/h).

This made the Triumph Bonneville the first production racer to achieve a 100mph lap. Uphill's second lap was even faster at 100.37mph (161.53km/h). He eased off on the final lap, wanting to ensure the machine finished, and achieved a final race average speed of 99.99mph (160.91km/h). In recognition of his achievement, Dunlop christened their K81 tyre the 'TT100', a name it still carries today. This was really the crowning achievement of the 650cc unit Triumph, gained at what many people consider to be its peak, and using a machine that was very close to standard.

7 Technical Description and Development

The Triumph 'B' series 650cc twins, which arrived on the market with their completely new engines and frames in 1963, were continuously developed throughout their lives. Triumph's development programme was based on three main inputs: fixing faults discovered in the product, production engineering changes to ease manufacture, and feeding in improvements discovered as a result of testing and racing. While the sum total of the improvements was significant, making the final models much improved, the year-on-year improvements were usually small and this tended to make it look as if the only significant changes to the range every year were to the colour schemes.

So the bikes went through the usual British bike evolution process, with incremental changes being applied annually until something approaching perfection was reached. In the case of the 'B' series twins, it is generally acknowledged that this peak was reached with the 1968 to 1970 model years, resulting in a fine performing machine with excellent handling. The proof of the pudding came with the 1969 Isle of Man TT production race win by a Bonneville at 99.99mph (160.91km/h) and the first 100mph lap at the TT by a production bike. The 'B' series was relaunched in 1970 for the 1971 model year with all-new running gear developed by the BSA development centre at the infamous Umberslade Hall. The new range of BSA and Triumph twins shared their running gear, but the Triumph engine did not initially fit the new frame and the seat height was far too high for smaller riders. Desperate development work at Meriden 'on the job' found a means of fitting the engines. The seat height issues were addressed by lowering the suspension and taking padding out of the seat before a permanent cure was found by lowering the seat rails. Despite the collapse of Triumph's parent company BSA in 1973 and the Meriden blockade, the 'B' series twin was stretched to 750cc and remained in production (on and off) until 1988, when production finally ended at Les Harris's facility in Newton Abbot, Devon.

The technical sections below look at the engine development in terms of the initial 650cc bikes, then the 750cc derivatives and the 8-valve TSS. The sections addressing the running gear look firstly at the pre-1971 items, and then the post-1971 oil-in-frame (OIF) components.

Engine Layout and Design

The original 650cc twin engine was based closely on both the layout and dimensions of the pre-unit engine. Some items, such as the valve-gear design and geometry, were carried over unchanged – after all, when you already have a good thing, why change it? The main reason for producing a 'unitized' engine was to cut down weight, complexity and, of course, costs. Also unit construction was perceived as being modern in the buying public's mind. Triumph was only too aware of this trend, having introduced its unit-construction single, the Terrier/Tiger Cub in 1953 and the 350cc twin Twenty-one in 1957. So the last pre-unit engine in the range had to 'go unit' and 1963 was the year it would happen.

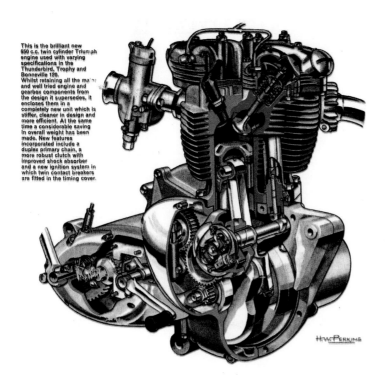

This is the brilliant new 650 c.c. twin cylinder Triumph engine used with varying specifications in the Thunderbird, Trophy and Bonneville 120. Whilst retaining all the main and well tried engine and gearbox components from the design it supersedes, it encloses them in a completely new unit which is stiffer, cleaner in design and more efficient. At the same time a considerable saving in overall weight has been made. New features incorporated include a duplex primary chain, a more robust clutch with improved shock absorber and a new ignition system in which twin contact breakers are fitted in the timing cover.

LEFT: The unit 650cc twin retained the layout of the pre-unit engine, with fore and aft camshafts driven by gears from the crankshaft. With the gearbox housed in the timing-side casting, the engine was compact and rigid.

BELOW: The 650cc engine had a one-piece crankshaft, with a central flywheel fixed in position with three bolts. Roller and ball main bearings supported the crank, and shell big-end bearings had their oil fed from the timing-side end of the crankshaft.

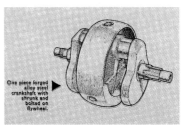

One piece forged alloy steel crankshaft with shrunk and bolted on flywheel.

The new Triumph engine had a one-piece crank, with a separate bolt-on flywheel positioned between the two big-end journals. This was fixed in position with three radial bolts and the bolts were locked in place using Loctite, a high-performance adhesive that replaced mechanical locking devices such as spring washers. The crank was supported on two main bearings: a roller type on the drive side to carry the drive loads, and a ball race on the timing side. The oil supply to the big ends was pumped through oilways in the crankcase via the outer timing cover and into the end of the crank. An oil seal in the timing cover kept the pressure up and the oil was fed into a gallery in the crank. There was a sludge trap incorporated in the gallery, and this performed the main oil filtering in the engine, before the oil made its way to the big ends. The soft metal shell big-end bearings were carried in H-section RR56 alloy conrods, which incorporated steel bearing end caps and used two high-tensile bolts to fix the matched end caps to the rod. The rods were highly polished to remove any stress points. The small ends were bushed, and the domed alloy pistons had cut-outs for the valves and had three rings: two compression and one oil scraper.

The engine had separate rear inlet and front exhaust camshafts and these were gear-driven via an intermediate gear from the crankshaft. This gave very precise operation of the cams, a good point for engine tuners as it was possible to change just the inlet or the exhaust cam, or change the valve timing of each cam individually. The cams were carried in bushes in the crankcases. In line with Turner's philosophy of designing with a sharp pencil – making sure nothing was introduced unnecessarily – the inlet camshaft was used to drive the oil pump via the traditional Triumph sliding block on the timing side, and was hollow to provide the timed breather mechanism on the drive side, via a rotary valve. The breather vented to the outside via a tube tucked away in front of the gearbox casing. The exhaust camshaft carried the centrifugal advance and retard unit and the contact-breaker points on its timing side, and the tachometer drive on the drive side. This minimized the need for ancillary drives and helped to make the engine both light and simple.

The camshafts operated tappets held in round blocks that were located by screw-in pegs in the cast iron barrel. This was fixed to the crankcases by eight studs and nuts, and had a gap between the bores to assist cooling, although the pushrod tubes did their best to obstruct the airflow. The pushrods were encased in steel tunnels: the top and bottom sealing arrangements would change a number of times during the life of the engine to try to fix the oil leaks.

The light alloy head was bolted to the barrel with nine studs: four outer bolts that bolted directly through the head, four inner bolts that bolted through the rocker boxes and the head, and one middle stud that helped to seal between the bores. The cylinder head carried two valves per cylinder and two-part valve springs (inner and outer) were used. The valves sealed against hardened steel inserts that were cast in place in the cylinder head. The rockers and tappets that operated the valves were housed in two rocker boxes that were bolted onto the top of the head – one for the inlet valves and one for the exhaust valves. In addition to the two main head bolts, each box had five secondary fixings to help to fix them in position and stave off the oil leaks that can result from having the stressed rocker boxes: the valve cover end had three studs and nuts and the other end had two screws. The rockers were carried on a spindle and end float was taken up by a helical spring (Thackeray) washer. Tappets were threaded with locknuts to allow adjustment. Oil from the return side of the system was fed to the

rocker spindles through banjo unions on the ends of the spindle on the timing side, which were fixed in position with domed chromed nuts. The tappets were accessed through round tappet covers (renowned for unscrewing themselves) and valve clearances were adjusted using screw and locknuts. The head came in two castings for single or twin carburettors. The twin-carburettor head had screw-in carriers for each carburettor, angled outwards at the traditional Triumph 45 degrees, while the single-carburettor head had parallel ports and a bolt-on alloy two-branch manifold. The exhaust ports carried screw-in steel exhaust-pipe adaptors, over which the exhaust pipes fitted, and were fixed in place using finned chromed steel clamps.

The tachometer was driven directly (that is, at half engine speed) from the end of the exhaust camshaft, which meant the cable was screwed directly into the crankcases and then had to be bent through 90 degrees to snake its way up to the tachometer. As the camshaft revolved anti-clockwise, when viewed from the drive side of the engine, the tachometer cable and hence the tachometer itself also revolved anti-clockwise. This resulted in either a large loop of cable if directed outside the exhaust pipe, which made it vulnerable to snagging, or a very tight loop to pass the cable inside the pipes, which shortened the life of the cable considerably. This unsatisfactory system was replaced in 1966 by a small gearbox fixed to the crankcases, which turned the drive through 90 degrees, reversed the rotation of the cable to clockwise and reduced the gearing from direct to 2:1.

Engine breathing arrangements were carried over from the pre-unit models, with a mechanical breather comprising a timed rotary valve driven by the inlet camshaft. The valve was timed to open when the piston was on the downward stroke and closed on the upward stroke, giving a partial vacuum in the crankcases. The vent to the outside world emerged in front of the final-drive sprocket, and a pipe was used to direct any blowby. This system avoided pressurizing the cases, and hence cut down on the possibility of oil leaks. The system worked but was replaced in 1970 by a much simpler system.

The engine unit was pretty much right from the start. While there were some issues around camshaft wear, addressed throughout the unit's life with changes to the oil system and cured by nitrating the cams, and the inevitable vibration problems as more power was extracted, there were no fundamental flaws in the unit and it proved to be reliable and robust in service.

In 1965 Triumph introduced a new Top Dead Centre (TDC) location system to help set the ignition timing. This had a slot cut in the flywheel and positioned so that a pointer placed in a hole behind the cylinder block would lock the engine at TDC. The oil pressure indicator on the pressure release valve was deleted this year, eliminating a source of oil leaks. More improvements followed in 1966 to increase performance, address wear problems and increase oil tightness. A new flywheel was fitted, which was lighter than before at 2½lb (1.13kg), and the balance factor of the engine was maintained at 85 per cent by having a stepped edge to the flywheel. In conjunction the crankshaft was positively located by clamping it to the timing side main bearing. Oil feed to the tappets was improved to combat wear, and new straight-edged pushrod tubes were used, again to combat oil leaks. In the increasing battle against wear, especially to the camshaft, a revised oil feed to

The unit engine featured the rev counter driven from the end of the exhaust camshaft, small round tappet covers and (for 1970) an engine breather that vented into the chain case with a large diameter pipe at the top rear of the case to vent the gas.

the tappets was introduced in 1967, along with an improved oil pump with a higher scavenge capacity. For 1968 the tappet oil feed was again revised, and the cylinder head was retained using twelve pointed nuts: these gave much enhanced accessibility to the nuts, making it easier to torque them down accurately. The new Lucas 6CA contact breaker points were also introduced, which meant that the accurate timing of each cylinder could be set independently; with the 4CA set, as previously fitted, accurate timing on both cylinders could only be achieved by changing the points gap. The engine was maturing nicely, and all the detail changes meant that the unit was getting stronger and more oil-tight. The 1969 model year saw Triumph start to change to the UNF thread form as standard, the feed capacity of the oil pump was increased, and an electrical oil pressure switch was fitted to the front of the timing cover. The recurring camshaft wear problem was finally solved with the introduction of a nitrated camshaft – a surface treatment that prevents wear – early in the 1969 model year (from engine number DU87105), and the flywheel weight was increased.

One of the main changes to the 1970 engine was a major revision to the breathing system. The rotary valve breather driven by the inlet camshaft was deleted, and by removing the drive-side oil seal on the main bearing, the crankcases could breathe into the primary-chain case. The chain case was vented to the outside with a large-diameter pipe taken off the highest part of the back of the chain case, which was protected by a baffle-plate to minimize oil loss. This outlet was connected, via a T-piece to the oil tank breather, to a distinctive 'D'-shaped silver pipe that was clipped to the left-hand side of the rear mudguard, venting the pressure variations to the outside by the number plate. Three small-diameter (1/16in/1.6mm) holes were drilled in the wall of the crankcase at the level of the bottom run of the primary chain to maintain the primary-chain-case oil level at its correct level. This system worked and was much simpler than the previous one. It also meant that the primary chain case shares its oil with the engine and, as long as there is engine oil, will always be filled to the right level. The only downside is that use of some engine oils with friction modifiers can cause the clutch to slip.

Along with the introduction of the oil-in-frame running gear in 1971, the engines had to have a new cylinder head, specially machined to allow the fitment of the new rocker boxes that were needed to fit the engine in the new frame. The rocker boxes gained a small inspection hole in the side to enable a feeler gauge to be inserted from the side to ease the task of setting the tappets. These were retained on the 650cc motors until 1972, when new rocker boxes were introduced that replaced the round covers with a single flat cover for both tappets, giving greatly improved access.

Probably the major development of the 'B' series engine was its growth in capacity to 750cc. The need for a larger twin was driven from the US market, which still held the Triumph twin in high esteem and was not so keen on the 3-cylinder Trident. The US East and West Coast distributors had cobbled together the T120RT in 1970 to achieve homologation for a 750cc twin for flat-track racing, and were still clamouring for more. The T120RT was essentially a standard Bonneville with an aftermarket big-bore kit, and it was really close to the limit of what the engine's internal components could stand. Triumph initially looked at increasing the size of the 650 simply by boring out the existing 650cc engine, but Bert Hopwood's test programme revealed problems with crankshaft life, head gasket problems and vibration. A crash course of development was started in late 1971 and completed in April 1972. This resulted in an engine that retained the 650cc engine's 82mm stroke, but had a larger bore and a number of detailed changes to ensure the reliability of the bigger unit. The crank problems were addressed by ditching the 650's camshaft profiles and replacing

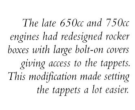
The late 650cc and 750cc engines had redesigned rocker boxes with large bolt-on covers giving access to the tappets. This modification made setting the tappets a lot easier.

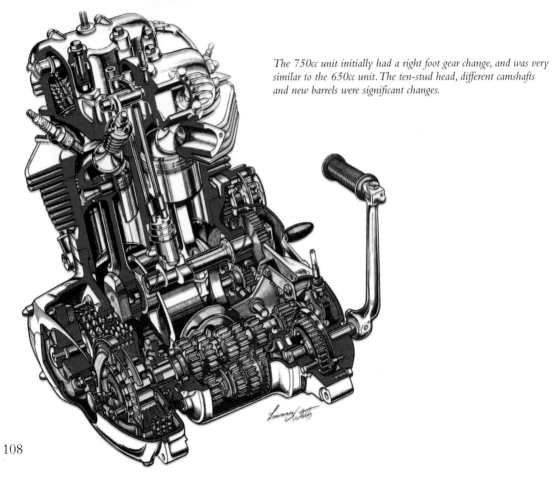

The 750cc unit initially had a right foot gear change, and was very similar to the 650cc unit. The ten-stud head, different camshafts and new barrels were significant changes.

them with a Spitfire profile inlet and a soft 1950s 6T profile exhaust. This change was combined with revised tappet foot radiuses, which changed the lift and hence gave softer power characteristics. The engine was further beefed up using stronger section conrods and a heavy-duty timing side main bearing. The connecting rods were shorter than the 650 rods, and the crank was given an easier time by reducing the compression ratio to 8.5:1 (or 8.6:1, according to some sources), down from the T120R's 9:1.

The barrels were also beefed up, and the crankcases were modified with a wider 'mouth' to accept them and strengthening around the main bearings. The head problems were solved by an additional centre fixing bolt. Despite its de-tuning in comparison to the 650cc unit, the revised engine produced a claimed 52bhp. Due to supply problems with the new barrel castings, the initial engines used the same castings as those for the 650cc engines, but with revised machining that allowed for the ten-stud fixing for the head but only a 75mm bore, giving a capacity of 724cc. This allowed the 724cc barrel to be rebored once, but there was not enough meat on the casting to allow for the 76mm bore that would give a full 744cc. After engine number XH 22018, the supply of new barrel castings started and the bore was increased to 76mm, raising the capacity to 744cc. The new ten-stud head had revised rocker boxes, with pegs for positive location and large bolt-on one-piece covers for the tappets. These killed two bugbears at once: now it was easy to set the valve clearances and the loss-prone small round rocker covers were consigned to history. However, sealing problems led to these covers being revised for 1974, with two extra fixing screws and revised gaskets. As a result of the softer cams, the 750's valve clearances were changed from the tight 2 thou inlet and 4 thou exhaust of the 650s to a loose 8 thou inlet and 6 thou exhaust; note that the exhaust clearance is actually smaller than the inlet on the 750cc engine, which is a result of the wildly different

profiles of the two camshafts and followers. All 750cc motors were equipped with the five-speed gearbox as standard. Triumph started to produce the new 750cc twins, the T140V Bonneville and TR7RV Tiger, in September 1972.

The T140V engine was largely unchanged until 1975, since the Meriden sit-in allowed only limited numbers of machines to be produced. The only major engine change introduced in 1976 (along with the change to left-foot gear change) was a new barrel casting that used UNF cylinder-head studs. A new head gasket was introduced for 1978, but the major change for that model year was the introduction of the T140E unit on 1 January 1978. This unit was designed to meet the latest US emissions requirements and was fitted with a new cylinder head with parallel inlet ports (slightly less efficient in terms of breathing, but giving better emissions), a revised engine breathing system with gases being recirculated into the air box, and Amal Concentric Mk2 carburettors, which were fitted to the new ports using rubber hoses. The power output of this modified unit was a claimed 49bhp (3bhp less than the T140V), which meant a slightly reduced top speed. Lucas Rita electronic ignition was also fitted, again to meet the emissions requirement tests by which the engine had to be run for a considerable distance without adjustment and then retested: the manual contact-breaker point ignition system could not stay in adjustment for the distance and the bike would have failed the test. The Lucas Rita system was 'fit and forget', and with its light-actuated triggering and electronic advance resulted in very accurate timing that did not slip out of adjustment. One quirk of the system was that it fired both plugs when it was first powered up – so if you'd kicked the bike over a few times before realizing the kill switch was off, there would be a massive backfire when the kill switch was turned on. The year 1980 saw the introduction of a new 4-valve oil pump, with secondary check ball valves fitted to both feed and scavenge sides of the pump, which removed the issue of grit in the oil holding open one of the valves. This meant a revised timing cover, with increased clearance for the fatter pump, although existing cases from earlier models can have alloy removed from their insides to give the clearance the later pump needs.

The next major change to the engine was the long-awaited electric start, introduced as an option on 2 April 1980. This comprised an Indian-built Lucas M3 starter motor (as used on the Triumph Tigress scooter in the 1960s), which was placed behind the cylinder block, underneath the carburettors. The starter drove the inlet camshaft pinion via a sprag clutch and a gear train housed in an extended timing cover. There were some slight problems with wrong oilways and weak gear teeth on the initial production models, but the starter does have a pretty good reputation. Sprag clutches can fail, and from time to time they are in short supply, but in general the starter is reliable and actually works. The positioning of the electric starter motor meant the TDC locator hole was repositioned in the front of the cases. The beefed-up electrics introduced in 1979 obviously helped in keeping the battery fully charged. The engine then carried on largely unchanged, as development effort was concentrated on the new 8-valve TSS unit.

The TSS engine was the only further development of the 750cc motor that Meriden was able to produce. The intention was to produce a stronger, better-breathing high-performance engine that could compete with the then current crop of Japanese 750cc bikes. The Co-op succeeded in this aim, and the TSS motor was, when not marred by quality problems with its individual components, a fast and competitive engine that retained Triumph's character. The bottom half of the engine featured an all-new crankshaft with narrower but larger diameter big-end journals (at 1.8765 to 1.8760in/47.6631 to 47.6504mm) than the previous 750cc motor (at 1.6235 to 1.6240in/41.237 to 41.25mm), and wider end-wall webs. This made for a stiffer crank, which was able to handle the increased power (a claimed 57bhp) of the TSS motor. The conrods were forged in RR56 aluminium and were longer than the 2-valve 750cc motor components to cope with the increased big-end diameter. As the engine's bore centres were further apart with the new barrels, this meant that the small ends in the connecting rods were offset by 3mm. The surface of the crank was fully machined, notionally to improve the engine's balance.

The barrels were all new and were made of cast aluminium with shrunk-in iron liners. This construction gave better cooling than the standard bikes' cast iron items, and of course was substantially lighter. Pistons were flat-topped to suit the more modern combustion chamber design. One odd thing that Triumph didn't do was to take the opportunity to get rid of the troublesome pushrod tubes and cast the tunnels into the barrel directly. The all-alloy cylinder head was also new and was based on the Weslake unit that was marketed as an aftermarket fitment by companies such as Morgo in the 1960s. The head carried four valves per cylinder, with the inlet valve heads being 1.152in (29.26mm) in diameter, and the exhaust valves had a slightly smaller diameter of 0.995in (25.273mm). The valves were operated by forked rockers that ran on rocker shafts mounted on pillars cast directly into the head, thus getting rid of Triumph's other top bugbear – separate rocker boxes. The two rocker covers, inlet and exhaust, were substantial finned castings that were secured directly to the head by six screws. The head itself was fixed to the barrel directly by four Allen screws and also by six through-studs that passed through the barrel and were screwed into the crankcases directly, giving a total of ten actual fixings. The two inner studs needed to have sealing rings placed between their washer and the head to avoid oil leaks. There were a further four short studs and nuts to secure the barrel to the crankcases. The rocker spindles had to

RIGHT: *The TSS was the ultimate development of Turner's twin. The 8-valve head increased power to a claimed 57bhp and this necessitated substantial improvements to the bottom end to cope with the power.*

BELOW: *The ancestry of the TSS can be traced back to the Weslake 8-valve head, marketed by Rickman in the 1960s. Here a unit Triumph engine with a Rickman top end is mounted in Rickman's-Metisse frame.*

be removed to allow access to the head retaining fixtures. The head-to-barrel joint was sealed using a pair of 'Cooper' sealing rings fitted at the top of each cylinder liner, rather than a conventional copper gasket.

The head featured a shallow angle between the valves and a central sparking plug, and had a 9.5:1 compression ration, up from the 7.9:1 of the T140E. The modern combustion chamber shape gave good combustion and limited detonation or 'pinking' when run on standard four-star fuel. Power output was a claimed 57bhp at 6,500rpm, a big increase on the standard 750cc bike.

Unfortunately the TSS was somewhat underdeveloped and was rushed into production before all the faults had been eliminated. Porous cylinder heads were common, causing extensive oil leakage and large warranty bills. This problem was compounded by some loose cylinder liners, which meant that blown head sealing rings were relatively common. While relatively easy to fix, these problems tarnished the engine's reputation. However, a sorted TSS is a brilliant bike, making it a fine final model of the 'B' Series twin series.

Primary Drive and Clutch

The unit 650 primary drive and clutch was fitted in the drive-side crankcase and covered with the polished primary chain case, which had a styling flash on its side and a cast-in 'Triumph' logo at the front. The alternator shared the space, with its rotor driven from the crankshaft and the stator mounted on studs on the crankcase face. The primary drive chain was a ⅜in, eighty-four link duplex item, and a slipper tensioner was fitted on the lower run – a good idea, but difficult to use as the lower frame rail got in the way, making a special tool necessary to operate it. Unlike the Triumph 350cc and 500cc 'C' series bikes, the adjuster was designed in from the start and was fitted in its entirety into the inner case, so the chain could be

adjusted without having to fit the outer case. Chain tension could be checked through a hole on the top of the crankcase casting, closed with a screw-in plug, and the orifice was also used to fill the case with oil. The clutch was a three-spring unit with twelve plates (six plain driven, and six bonded drive), which was up to the job and gave few problems. Clutch adjustment was by a screw-in clutch pressure plate, which was accessed through a screw-in cover on the outer face of the chain case. The clutch was activated by a pushrod that ran through the hollow gearbox mainshaft to the clutch operating mechanism on the gearbox outer cover on the timing side. This was a three-ball and ramp system, using three balls on a pair of steel pressings, that was actuated by the clutch cable and moved the clutch pushrod out to free the clutch.

The case gained a circular inspection hatch in 1968, fixed with three screws. This cover had the 'Triumph' logo cast in and gave access to timing marks: a pin was mounted on the case and a corresponding mark was made on the alternator rotor to enable the timing to be set precisely using a stroboscope.

The 750cc T140 introduced in 1973 saw a beefed-up primary drive, with a ⅜in pitch triplex chain replacing the duplex item fitted to the 650cc unit, and hence a new clutch basket and drive sprocket. The move to the left-foot gear change in 1976 meant changes to the primary chain case: a new hole appeared in it to take the gear change shaft, which now stretched across from the gearbox, with a crank in it to avoid the clutch, while the inspection cover that gave access to the alternator stator timing marks was replaced with a small screw-in cover – a cheaper solution that was also easier to make oil-tight. The cast-in 'Triumph' logo on the front of the case was reinstated.

Gearbox

The gearbox fitted to the first unit 650s was a positive-stop, four-speed unit, which was installed into a casing that was integral with the timing side of the crankcases. The performance of this gearbox was good, giving light lever action with positive gear selection, and was largely trouble free. An inner gearbox casing that carried the bearings for the timing side of the gearbox was bolted onto the end of the casing, and a further polished outer case carried the gear-lever and gear change, kick starter and clutch mechanisms. The gearbox was a traditional British design with concentric input and output via a mainshaft. The gears were carried on the mainshaft and a layshaft that sat below the mainshaft enabled the gearbox and hence the engine unit to be relatively short. The drive came into the gearbox via the clutch, which was mounted on a taper on the mainshaft. Drive was then directed through the various gears before it reached the drive sprocket, which was mounted on the mainshaft behind the clutch. The mainshaft was supported on ball races, while the lighter-loaded layshaft was supported on needle roller bearings. The gears were nickel steel and case hardened. The gear selection mechanism comprised a quadrant that moved two selector forks to engage and disengage the gears and was operated from the timing side. The quadrant position was fixed by a spring-loaded plunger that engaged in slots on the periphery of the quadrant. The kick-starter mechanism was in the gearbox outer case behind the two gearbox shafts, and drove a gear splined onto the mainshaft via a quadrant. The speedometer was driven off the end of the gearbox layshaft as it had been on the pre-unit bikes, until a rear-wheel-driven unit was specified for 1966.

The gearbox was right from the start and very few significant changes were made to it until 1968. The move to UNF threads resulted in a slightly longer mainshaft in 1968, and a change was made to the third-gear ratios in 1969. However, significant changes to the gearbox shaft dimensions were made from engine number CC15546, resulting in a loss of backwards compatibility on many gearbox components. Another significant change, and a retrograde one at that, came towards the end of the 1970 season, when at engine number ED52044 the plunger mechanism used to locate the gear change quadrant was replaced with a precision pressed spring. This was not only difficult to assemble, it also did not work anywhere near as well as the previous mechanism. This dodgy selector mechanism was replaced in the spring of 1973 when the box gained a T150 Trident-style cam plate and indexing plunger.

The gearbox was brought up to date in late 1971 for the 1972 season with the introduction of an optional five-speed unit. This followed the previous layout and is interchangeable. The additional gear enabled the gear ratios to be closer together, not something strictly needed by the torquey Triumph engine for street use, but necessary for facing up to the Japanese opposition and good for the production racers. The five-speed box was successful, it worked well without any real glitches and was fitted as standard to all the 750cc machines.

The next major change to the gearbox was in 1976, when the gear change was moved from the right-hand side to the left. This was achieved by incorporating a crossover shaft for the gear-change mechanism in the crankcases. The shaft ran across the width of the engine, between the gearbox casing and the crank housing. The shaft connected to the gear-change mechanism in the gearbox end housing and emerged through the middle of the primary chain case in front of the clutch. The shaft had a 'U'-shaped crank in it to clear the clutch in the primary chain case. A new gearbox end cover had the gear-lever hole deleted. This was a very neat and maintenance-free conversion that did not compromise Triumph's slick gear change. The last significant change to the gearbox came in 1979, when a switch was incorporated into the gear-change mechanism to operate the neutral warning light fitted in the T140E and TR7RV.

Carburettors

Several types of carburettor were used on the 'B' series twins, especially towards the end of the model's Meriden years. The main units used were both made by Amal: the range started off using the Monobloc in 1963, and switched to the Concentric in 1968. This was superseded in 1979 by the Amal Concentric Mk2, which lasted until the final year of the T140E and ES models in the 1982 model year. The previous year (1981) saw the introduction of German-made Bing Constant Velocity (CV) carburettors on the Executive models, so enabling the venerable engine to meet the ever stricter US emissions laws. The CV Bings were standard on all US models (T140E, ES, Executive and Royal) and the TSX for the 1982 model year.

The Amal Monobloc was an innovatory design when it first appeared in the 1950s as it had its float bowl incorporated into the main casting – hence the name. This meant that there were no leak-prone joints between the float chamber and the main carburettor, and it also meant that the float height was fixed, removing a problem area for amateur engine tuners.

One slight problem with the Monobloc was that the adjustment screws (pilot jet and throttle stop) were on the opposite side to the float bowl cover. While this was not a problem with a single carburettor set-up, with twin carburettors it meant that the adjusters or the float bowl would be difficult to access. This problem was alleviated to a certain extent by making 'handed' carburettor bodies, although this was an expensive policy as it meant a completely different casting for each side. The Bonneville was always listed as having handed Monoblocs. The Monobloc acquired a good reputation, being easy to set up and tune, and reliable in service. The side mounting of the float bowl cover and the bottom-mounted main jet cover nut meant that any foreign bodies or water in the carburettor could be quickly sorted out at the roadside. Amal came under pressure from Triumph to produce a cheaper instrument, however, resulting in the Concentric in 1968. This model was so-called because the float was at the bottom of the carburettor and the main jet projected down into the float chamber. The float chamber cover was fixed to the bottom of the main body, and the main body casting was designed so that the holes for the tuning screws could be drilled on either side, so providing left- or right-handed models using the same casting. This cut costs and solved the access problems of the Monobloc, and handed Concentrics were fitted to the Bonneville.

When introduced the Concentric did have some problems, since bikes would often stall when pulling up as the concentric design caused fuel starvation. This was fixed by changes to the pilot jet drillings. The instrument also gained a reputation for rapid wear, especially between the slide and main body, which made it difficult to tune correctly. This is still an issue and it is generally advisable to fit chrome-plated slides to reduce wear to a minimum. However, the Concentric was cheap (and still is), relatively easy to maintain and did the job.

The Amal Concentric Mk2 was fitted to the T140E. This was a development of the original Concentric Mk1, with a new square-styled body and a built-in enriching device for cold starts, which dispensed with the traditional tickler – and the smell of petrol on a Bonneville rider's gloves! The Tiger stayed with the Concentric Mk1 as it was not exported to the USA after 1979. German-made Bing Constant Velocity (CV) carburettors were fitted to all the 1982 US models – the Bonneville, Executive and Royal – to meet stricter emissions legislation, but in the UK market they equipped just the Royal and Executive. The Harris bikes were fitted with the Amal Concentric Mk1½ (essentially a Mk1 Concentric equipped with the enriching device from the Mk2 that replaced the tickler), thus making sure that no petrol leaked out and so keeping within the stricter emissions laws introduced in the UK and Europe.

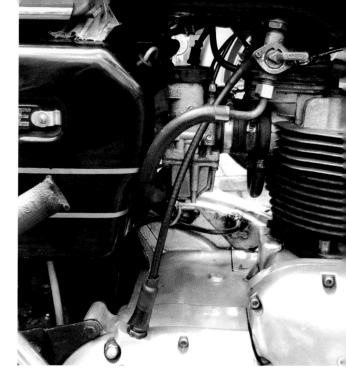

LEFT: The Amal Concentric was introduced in 1968. The splayed head was retained and the characteristic lines of the Triumph engine are illustrated by this 1970 example.

ABOVE: The T140E (for 'emissions') saw the introduction of Amal Concentric Mk2 carburettors on parallel inlet ports. The Mk2s had a built-in choke mechanism, which meant the tickler was no more.

Frame and Swinging Arm

The new unit-construction engine was significantly shorter than the previous separate engine and gearbox, and Triumph took the opportunity to produce a completely new frame for the new range. The last of the pre-unit 650s had a twin down-tube frame, which, while looking good and well received by the public, had significant faults on its introduction that necessitated additional strengthening to its headstock, and also featured a poorly braced swinging arm. The handling and roadholding of this frame, while not bad, was nowhere near as good as Norton's Featherbed or indeed BSA's A65 unit, both of which were one-piece, all-welded designs.

The design of the new frame was overseen by Triumph designer Brian Jones. Following the theme set by Triumph's other model ranges, the all-new frame was made up in two parts: a front loop and rear sub-frame. One myth perpetuated in the classic bike press is to confuse the frame on the 650 twins with that of the 350 and 500cc 'C' series twin frames. The 650 frame never had an unbraced 'swan neck' type headstock or an unsupported swinging arm pivot. The unit constriction 'B' series frame design benefited from the knowledge gained in the development of the 'C' series frame, and did not display any of the flaws that existed in the early 3TA and 5TA frames. The frame used in the 650s had a steering head that was properly triangulated from the start of production with a top tube and lower top tube used to produce a very rigid headstock, and the swinging arm pivot was always well supported by the rear engine plates. The basic design of the 650cc bikes' frame was sound and did not change until

The first-generation T120 frame was of brazed lug construction and was pretty much right from the word go. Some tweaks to the steering head angle and some stiffening led to a world-class handler.

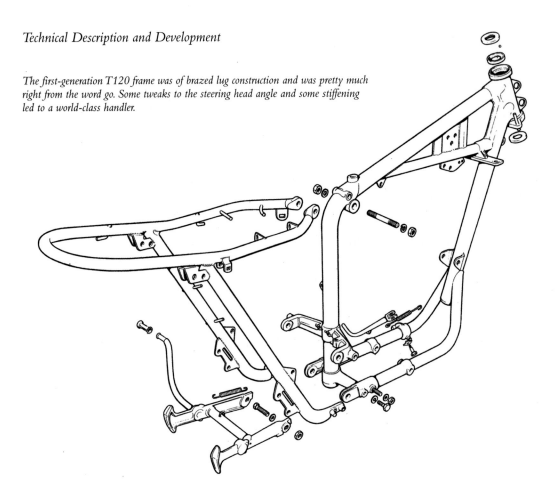

the advent of the Umberslade Hall-designed oil-carrying trellis. The 'B' series frame did, however, undergo a series of detailed improvements that improved its handling and roadholding until it was accepted as one of the best that the British bike industry produced. The front loop was of brazed lug and tube construction, while the rear sub-frame was all welded. The front loop had a single tube making up the seat tube and top tube that was brazed into the cast headstock. A second smaller diameter tube ran back from the headstock to the rear of the top tube to triangulate the steering head, making it rigid, and a single down-tube swept downwards from the headstock. This tube had two tubes welded to it at its base, and these spread out horizontally to form the duplex tube engine cradle. The two engine cradle tubes terminated

in a cast-iron bottom lug, which was also fixed to the base of the vertical seat tube, and carried the bolt-on fixings for the lower rear sub-frame. A couple of inches above this lug was the swinging arm fixing lug, a 'U'-shaped affair that located the ends of the swinging arm. The rear sub-frame was made up of a top loop to support the seat and mount the top of the rear shock absorbers, and twin tubes running from the top shock absorber mounts down to the back of the engine cradle. These two parts were bolted together, with the two top rails of the rear sub-frame bolting onto the rear of the top rail with a single stud, and each rear downtube bolted to the rear engine cradle with two bolts per side. The cast-iron headstock and tube geometry gave a steering angle of 65 degrees. The front footrests were fixed to fittings on the engine cradle and ran outside of the exhaust pipes, while the pillion footrests were mounted on triangular plates that were bolted onto the rear sub-frame. These plates also supported the silencers. The rear swinging arm was of conventional twin-sided design and was constructed of welded tubular steel. It was pivoted on two bronze bushes that pivoted on a spindle fitted between two lugs on the swinging arm lug. The outer ends of the swinging arm spindle were bolted through and supported by the rear engine plates, providing a great degree of rigidity to the rear end. The swinging arm bushes had to be line-reamed to fit the spindle, and regular greasing was needed to prevent wear.

The Triumph's frame was a simple, rigid and fundamentally correct structure that, with development work to address vibration, handling and roadholding by Doug Hele, was to remain in production until 1970.

For 1964 the frame remained much the same, but the front footrest mounts on the lower engine cradle were deleted, with the engine plates modified to carry bolt-on footrests. While this modification gave increased ground clearance for cornering, and also meant the footrests did not need to be removed to get the exhaust pipes off, the main reason it was done was to cut down the vibration getting through to the rider. Again there were only slight changes in 1965, the main one being the fitting of a steering lock. The lock fitted into a lug on the side of the headstock and engaged with a slot cut in the fork stem. The swinging arm fixing bolt, which was originally extracted from the left-hand side, was modified so that it was extracted from the right-hand side to ease access.

The most significant improvement to the 650's frame was made in 1966, when Doug Hele, Triumph's chief designer under Bert Hopwood, oversaw a series of modifications that was to bring the big Triumph range's handling up to scratch. The most significant was the reduction of the steering head angle from 65 degrees to 62 degrees; it was no coincidence

that this was the same head angle as Norton's famous Featherbed frame, the benchmark for handling at the time. When combined with some modifications to the ride height and damping of the front forks, his simple modification gave a significant improvement to the high-speed steering, bringing the frame up to the standards of its rivals. In addition, the opportunity was taken to fix fairing lugs (two horizontal round tubes) to the new head lug. A new wider swinging arm, with the timing side arm moved out by ¼in (6.4mm), was fitted to the rear.

The changes made to the 1966 frame had improved the handling to a level comparable with the opposition and the design carried on almost unchanged into the 1967 model year. The only change was the repositioning of the steering lock from the headstock to the top yoke of the forks. This meant a small modification to the headstock with a small lug being added to provide a location hole for the steering lock pin. The new front lug also had new steering stops fitted to allow for different, slimmer fuel tanks.

For 1968 attention was paid to the rear end of the frame, with thicker tube used for the swinging arm (12swg rather the previous 14swg) and larger corner fillets were used. These modifications were made to increase the rigidity of the rear end, and succeeded, giving another boost to the roadholding of the bike. The long curved side-stand, much more stable than the shorter 'foot' type previously fitted, was also introduced. A new swinging arm lug and head lug were introduced, the latter with an extended 'shelf' to prevent the steering lock from being engaged unless the forks were turned to full left lock. The rear frame had spigots incorporated on the left-hand side tube to support a new side panel on rubber mounts. The frame continued in this form through 1969.

The final version of the bolt-up, brazed lug frame was produced for the 1970 model year. The most significant change that was made was the introduction of two small triangular front engine plates, which were fixed to the lower front down-tube by two bolts, and with a single stud fixing to the engine. The main reason for this was production expediency – it made it a lot easier to slot the engine into the frame on the production line – but it also helps the mechanic to remove and replace the engine. This feature provides an easy recognition feature for 1970 machines. The only other change for 1970 was the introduction of an adjustable stop for the prop stand.

The Triumph's complete frame and running gear was changed in 1971 with the introduction of the Umberslade Hall-designed common frame for BSA and Triumph twins. In comparison with the Triumph frame with its two-piece construction, single down-tube and brazed lug construction, the new frame was a more modern design, featuring all-welded construction and duplex front down-tubes. Its main distinguishing feature was the oil being carried in the frame. The oil was carried in a large diameter 'L'-shaped tube that formed the top tube and seat tube of the frame, running from the headstock, under the fuel tank and then curving downwards to the back of the engine. The base of the tube was sealed off with a flat plate containing a sump plate, gauze filter and drain plug. According to popular opinion the new frame led to a reduced oil capacity; the factory literature states a capacity of 5 (British) pints, the same capacity as Triumph's separate oil tank of the mid-1960s, although in reality the capacity is usually found to be more than 4 pints but less than 5 pints. There is a possible explanation for this apparently retrograde step. Originally it was planned to have the oil filler at the top of the big tube, just behind the headstock, but in production it was positioned under the nose of the dual seat, in order to provide adequate space for frothing and expansion of the oil. This resulted in the oil capacity of the frame being reduced from a planned 6 to 7 pints to around 4½ to 5 pints. It has been suggested

that the filler was not positioned behind the headstock because the factory was afraid that riders would mistake it for the petrol filler or that passing vandals would deposit rocks in the oil tank – but the positioning of the oil filler on the contemporary oil-in-frame unit singles in this position indicates that this was probably just a rumour.

Twin tubes dropped from the headstock down to cradle the engine and then were joined to each side of the base of the oil-bearing tube. The swinging arm was supported on two solid bushes with good support to swinging arm ends provided by welded-on end plates. The welded-on rear sub-frame comprised a horizontal loop to support the seat, and twin tubes running from the base of the oil-bearing main spine up to the rear shock mounts. The frame was considered to be a good handler with excellent roadholding, and the design was used for the Meriden and Les Harris Triumph Bonneville and Tiger until production of these models ended in 1988. The new frame meant that the air filter assembly was also new. It comprised a pair of light alloy castings that wrapped around the oil-tank tube and carried two separate air filters on either side. The two castings formed an air chamber and carried the air filter, and were covered by outer alloy castings that incorporated a fake ribbed 'air intake' moulding on their outer edge, air for the filters being fed in via the inside edge of the inner castings. The single-carburettor models had a central air intake incorporated in the middle of these castings, while the twin-carburettor Bonneville had its air intakes incorporated into the outer edge of the central castings and the inner edge of the outer casing, with the carburettor being fed its clean air through rubber tubes. Behind the air-cleaner housing there were small triangular steel pressings, with the right-hand side one carrying the ignition switch.

One connection with the past that was lost with the introduction of the new frame was the replacement of the traditional Triumph

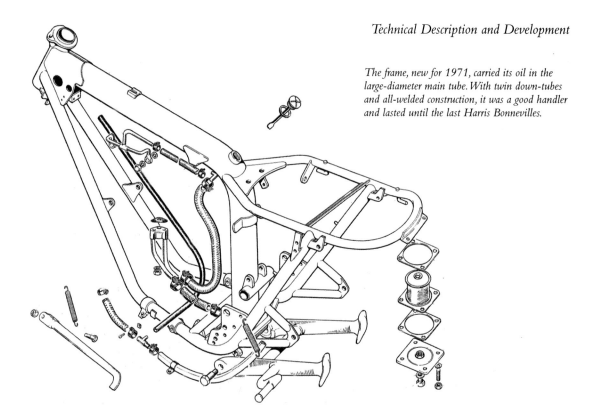

The frame, new for 1971, carried its oil in the large-diameter main tube. With twin down-tubes and all-welded construction, it was a good handler and lasted until the last Harris Bonnevilles.

rear pillion footrests, used since the 1930s, by the round BSA pattern items. Triumph's pre-1971 pillion footrests were made from a flat steel forging, with the footrest pivoting around a special recessed screw, with its movement stiffened by a sprung washer. The flat, oval section footrest rubber had the Triumph logo moulded into it, and the whole assembly was of much higher quality (and a lot more expensive to produce) than BSA's units. These were cheaply made from steel pressings, their pivot was a simple standard bolt, and the round footrest rubbers were unmarked other than with some non-slip ribbing. However, there were faults with the Triumph design: the pivot would wear quickly in use, for example, allowing the footrest to drop down, and it could be fiddly to replace the spring washer with a new one. It needed to be fixed, though, as the one on the right side would then get in the way of the kick starter. Also, as wear set in, the footrests would no longer sit level when down but

would droop, making it easy for the pillion's feet to slide off them. This was caused by wear in both the footrest pedal and hanger, and meant replacement of the whole unit. The BSA footrests were much less prone to loosening off and flopping down than the Triumph units, and were easy to tighten up if they did. This, then, was a good example of improving the breed with a more economical and practical fitting – but they did not look as nice as the Triumph units!

The new frame was not without its problems. While its handling and roadholding was excellent, the seat height was a claimed 32in (813mm) but was nearer 34in (864mm) – in fact *Cycle World*'s test of May 1971 measured it at 34.5in (876mm). While the press did not make too big a deal of this 'feature', it was mentioned and the factory was aware of the problem. This issue was accentuated by the width of the seat and fuel tank, and short-legged riders did experience problems getting both feet down on the ground. Initially stop-gap actions were carried out, including short-ening the fork stanchions and removing padding from the seat, but the eventual solu-tion was to re-site the rear sub-frame seat loop tubes to a lower position on the oil tank, drop-ping the seat height to a more manageable 32in (813mm) for 1972 models – measured by *Cycle World* in its June 1972 test as 32.3in (820mm). This modification meant that the air cleaner casing that fitted around the oil tank tube was also modified, leading to compatibil-ity problems with the early frame ancillaries. The modified frame was introduced at frame number GG50414.

A second problem was the frame fracturing around the swinging arm mounts on the oil-bearing main tube. This was traced to inadequate main stand fixings, and the problem was com-pounded if the owner kick-started the bike while it was still on the main stand, which, as the seat height was too tall for short riders, was a not uncommon custom. Revised main stand lugs solved the problem.

Once these two faults were addressed, further developments to the frame were limited to

detail improvements, and the frame remained broadly unchanged until the final models were produced by Les Harris.

Front and Rear Suspension

When the unit twins were introduced, they carried over the same design of front forks as used on the pre-unit models. These two-way damped forks were designed with internal springs and were fitted from frame number DU101 to DU5824. With the springs enclosed in the stanchions the forks were slimmer than the subsequent versions, and the lower part of the Thunderbird's nacelle matched the diame-ter of the steel shrouds that covered the gap between the bottom yoke and the fork sliders. The TR6 and T120 had slim black rubber gaiters covering the stanchions.

The external spring-type forks were intro-duced on all bikes in the range in 1964, which meant that there were larger diameter and longer oil-seal holders, which were also used to positively locate the bottom of the springs. The stanchions were the same diameter as the inter-nally sprung units formerly fitted. The new forks

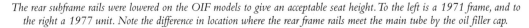

The rear subframe rails were lowered on the OIF models to give an acceptable seat height. To the left is a 1971 frame, and to the right a 1977 unit. Note the difference in location where the rear frame rails meet the main tube by the oil filler cap.

still provided two-way damping through oil-ways drilled in the stanchions, but had a larger oil capacity than the internal spring type. The Bonneville and Trophy models from 1964 sported larger rubber gaiters over the springs while the Thunderbird had new, larger-diameter tubular steel shrouds covering the springs. The diameter of these shrouds was larger than the upper section of the nacelle fork covers and introduced a 'step' in the diameter of the front forks just below the lower yoke, which resulted in the loss of the smoothness of line found with the 1963 nacelle. The Thunderbird kept the nacelle and fork shrouds until it was discontinued in 1966.

As part of Doug Hele's handling improvements, the front fork spring preload was reduced

After 1963 internal spring forks were replaced with stronger external spring items. The 1970 front forks were at the peak of their development, with two-way damping by shuttle valves and external springs covered by rubber gaiters.

by ¼in (6.4mm), which in conjunction with frame modifications helped to lower the centre of gravity of the bike forward and improved high-speed stability. The final improvement to the original forks was the introduction of the 'shuttle valve' two-way damping system, based on the Daytona-winning 'C' series 500cc twins. This was introduced for the 1968 model year, and comprised new stanchions with a series of small holes drilled in their circumference and a sliding valve in their base; these valves closed on the downward stroke of the forks, restricting the flow of oil and hence increasing damping effect, but opened on the rebound, allowing the forks to recover quickly to their normal state. The system was simple and effective, and gave much improved roadholding and a much more sophisticated ride. The forks were able to cope with rough or bumpy road surfaces much better than the previous types, giving a smoother ride and cutting down pattering. The development of the correct size and positioning of the holes took a great deal of meticulous experimentation by Hele and Triumph's famous tester Percy Tait before the optimum configuration was found. The forks were further modified in 1969, when the centres between the fork legs were increased from 6½in (16.5cm) to 6¾in (17.2cm) to allow for a wider front tyre.

With the introduction of the Umberslade-designed frame a new 'Ceriani'-type fork, with internal springs and alloy sliders, was introduced. These forks had exceptionally clean lines and looked much more modern than the previous types with their black-painted steel sliders and external springs covered by rubber gaiters.

The 1973 model year sliders were highly polished alloy and the rib was deleted. No fork bushes were fitted to the forks: the stanchions ran directly in the legs. While this seems unwise, the forks do seem to last very well, with the stanchions tending to wear rather than the alloy sliders. The design featured exposed chromed stanchions with small rubber dust seals to protect the oil seals, and the steering head boasted

tapered roller bearings, rather the previous ball and cups. The forks were two-way damped, had 6.74in (171mm) of travel and certainly looked up to date. Their performance was considered good by the journalists of the day and in service they have proved to be long-lasting and trouble-free. For the first two years of production the alloy sliders had a rough cast finish with a raised ridge about 5mm wide and a polished surface running down the length of the slider, but from 1973 the ridge was deleted and the complete surface of the slider was polished. A friction-type steering damper was listed, but few bikes seem to have had one fitted. Handlebars were rubber mounted using the bushes in the top yoke supporting the traditional Triumph single-bolt 'P'-shaped fixing brackets. A steering lock was standard, and was mounted in the centre front of the top yoke, where it was easy to access.

One problem was the ease with which these forks could twist. By utilizing a four-stud fitting to secure a cap to fix each side of the front wheel axle to the bottom of the fork leg, Umberslade claimed that the fork was as stiff as those that had gone before and there was no need for a bracing strut at the top of the fork sliders. Despite the factory's protestations, however, the fork was far too flexible and the front wheel could be deflected from its path relatively easily. The reason for this apparent design flaw may have been a styling and cost issue, since the front mudguard was supported on rubber-mounted wire stays that looked good, carried on the theme of lightness given by the headlamp support wires and was no doubt cheap to produce, but did not provide any bracing to the top of the fork sliders. The first fix was to incorporate a second wire fixing to the front mudguard, which helped to stop the original design from breaking but did not add much rigidity. This was only a temporary fix and the later Triumph twins from 1973 had a redesigned front mudguard with a substantial bracing strut fitted between the fork sliders, along with a lower rear mounting bracket that bolted onto the rear of the axle caps. However, these improvements were only used on the disc-braked models, the 750cc Bonneville and Tiger initially and only on the very last 650cc T120 Bonneville. Meanwhile the 650cc models were left to wither on the vine with little or no further development past the introduction of the 750s. Rubber bellows were fitted to protect the fork stanchions from dirt and grime to UK models from 1973, but the US models retained their exposed stanchions in the name of fashion.

The Harris Bonnevilles, produced between 1984 and 1988, had Italian-made Paioli-sourced front forks, which had a push-in axle rather than the bolt-on caps, and a stainless steel mudguard mounted on a centre bracket that doubled up as a fork brace.

On the original brazed lug construction frame, the rear suspension was provided by the phosphor-bronze bushed swinging arm, with Girling shock absorbers, giving approximately 3in (76mm) of movement. These units had three spring preload positions, enabling the rider to increase spring loading. Initially the springs and damper rods of the shock absorbers were fully enclosed with black-painted top shrouds and chrome-plated lowers, but as the 1960s marched on the enclosures got smaller and the exposed rear springs were chrome plated, until in 1969 the enclosures vanished for good. This styling 'improvement' led to reduced life for the units as the damper rod was exposed to road dirt, which caused corrosion and damage to the oil seals.

The rear swinging arm was modified in 1968, with a bobbin-type bearing that no longer needed to be line reamed when replaced; these necessitated a new frame lug at each end of the swinging arm to accommodate them.

The exposed spring Girling rear shocks were retained for the new 1971 Umberslade frame, but wheel travel was actually reduced to 2.5in (64mm), a retrograde step. The swinging arm was supported on phosphor-bronze bushes and there was provision for greasing the swinging arm pivots. The swinging arm pivot fitted into a tube welded to the back of the frame's oil-bearing tube, and the swinging arm pivoted around the spindle. Two steel-backed bushes were fitted at each end of the swinging arm. These were pre-sized, and new ones did not need to be reamed to size. The ends of the swinging arm pivot were supported by plates welded to the frame, unlike the previous frame where a frame lug was used, and the new frame's engine plates had holes in them to clear the swinging arm spindle. This made for a very rigid assembly and the engine plates did not need to be disturbed when changing the bushes. The Harris bikes retained the same swinging arm design, but used Italian Paioli rear units that gave three spring preloaded positions, just as the previous Girling units had.

Brakes and Wheels

The front brakes fitted to all the new unit models in 1963 were 8in (203mm) diameter single leading shoe units, as had been fitted to the pre-unit models since 1961. The full-width cast-iron hub used straight spokes radiating out from holes drilled around each side of the drum, and a chromed steel rim, the Bonneville and Thunderbird having 18in rims, while the Trophy boasted a 19in. The brake had a plain alloy backplate and fully floating shoes, but while they looked substantial the width of the brake shoes was only just over 1in (26mm) giving limited braking performance. A pressed-on circular chrome plate covered the other side of the hub. The brake's lack of ability to deal with the performance of the bike was recognized by Triumph, and as performance increased so the brake underwent steady development.

The first development, introduced at frame number DU24875 for the 1966 season, meant increasing the width of the brake lining to around 1½in (38mm), giving a substantial increase in braking area over the previous brake. The front hub was modified to accommodate the increase in width and is easily distinguished from the previous hub by the flange on the brake side to carry the spokes, which now needed a 90 degree bend at their base to fit. The flange allowed the braking area in the hub to be extended almost to the edge of the hub, and the alloy brake backplate did not cover the flange. This brake remained unchanged for 1967, but the 1968 model year saw the first incarnation of what is widely regarded as the best front drum brake made by any British manufacturer. Using

The 8in full-width single leading shoe front brake with its flanged hub was a significant improvement over the previous unit.

slightly wider 1⅜in (41mm) brake shoes and the 8in (203mm) flanged drum, a new light alloy brake plate was designed that incorporated twin leading shoes and a decent side air scoop to assist in cooling the brake. The twin leading shoe mechanism used external linkages, with the brake cable pulling on the front lever, which was linked via an adjustable rod to the rear lever. The two levers each operated a single brake shoe, making both act as 'leading' shoes: the self-servo action of the friction of the shoe pushing against the drum meant that the shoe is 'pulled' onto the drum by the drum's rotation. This decreases the effort needed to operate the brake. With a single leading shoe brake, a single cam operates both brake shoes. This gives one leading shoe and one trailing shoe. The trailing shoe needs much more force applied to it than the leading shoe to give the same braking performance, so the overall effort needed to operate a SLS unit is greater than a TLS unit.

This brake was a really good performer, with a very efficient design of the operating linkages, and excellent cooling via the large air scoop, covered with a chromed wire gauze to keep foreign bodies out, and an efficient extraction slot to the rear of the plate. The first iteration of the design did have a couple of faults, centred on the operating mechanism. The cable had to be long, as it connected to the back rear of the brake plate, and the length meant the operation of the brake was a bit on the spongy side. This was exacerbated on the US market models as their high handlebars meant the cable had to be some 5in (127mm) longer than the UK models. The length of the cable and its run also meant it was prone to being caught in the front mudguard, so that the brake could then be jammed on. This fault was fixed by putting a cable guide on the guard, but it was then found that the cable could jump out of the abutment in the backplate. This was righted by drilling the plate to allow a split pin (or cotter pin for the USA) to be fitted, which closed off the slot that the cable ran through.

In the light of these issues the brake operating mechanism was redesigned for 1969. The new mechanism, known as the 'bell crank', allowed for a shorter cable and a straighter run, with the cable following the line of the front fork legs with its abutment on the top of the plate. The new cranked operating arms were still connected by an adjustable arm, and the brake's efficiency was unchanged, but the shorter cable and more direct run made for a better feel to the brake. One point about the brake: at a standstill it is possible to pull the brake-lever back to the bars, which makes it feel as if there is far to much slack in the system, but when in motion the brake's operation really sharpens up, and the self-servo action of the brake makes it work with very little lever movement. Along with the modifications to the brake, the new brake cable was also fitted with a pressure switch to operate the brake light, a real safety benefit.

The brake continued unchanged in 1970, but was discontinued with the introduction of the new frame and running gear for 1971.

Note that in 1968 Triumph made available 'brake kits' to retrofit the newly introduced 1968 TLS front brake to 'update' unsold 1967 models.

The rear brake really did not change very much throughout the lifetime of the separate oil-tank models. The Triumph Quickly Detachable rear wheel was offered as an option throughout the life of pre-oil-in-frame model 650s. This option made it possible to remove the rear wheel without disturbing the rear brake or chain. The rear wheel was splined onto a combined rear brake drum and sprocket, and fixed in place by the rear-wheel spindle. Removing the rear spindle, the speedo drive and a spacer, meant the rear wheel could be released from the spline in the hub, and hence be removed to fix a puncture or change a rear tyre. While uncommon on US export models, this was a popular and practical option on UK models. The rear brake was operated by a rod, and the change of footrests in 1964 saw a new rear brake pedal, with a kinked brake rod

For 1968 came what was probably the best drum brake ever fitted to a British production machine. This 1968-model brake has non-standard operating arms, but shows the original configuration with the long cable sweeping in from the rear of the brake plate.

that ran outside of the rear sub-frame tube and inboard of the rear suspension unit. This was unsatisfactory as it made the brake feel very spongy, so it was replaced for 1965 with a straight rod that ran inboard of the rear sub-frame tube and suspension unit. This improved the feel of the brake and the design remained largely unchanged until the 1971 model year.

As described above, the brakes and running gear of the Triumph 650s were changed completely in the 1971 model year, with the introduction of the Umberslade-designed frame. The new all-alloy conical hubs were similar in appearance (if not in performance) to the Norton Manx units of the 1950s. The rear brake was an adequate 7in (178mm) in diameter, rod-operated on the left-hand side of the bike as before, and seems to have aroused little enthusiasm or enmity during its life. The front was an

8in (203mm) twin-leading shoe unit, described as fade-free in the contemporary literature but generally described as comical when tested to its limit!

There is no doubt that the brake was not as good as the Triumph twin-leading shoe that preceded it, but there is also a degree of folklore and legend dictating that the brake was worse than it really was. There is no doubt that the same brake on the Trident was out of its depth – conversely using it on the T25SS Blazer 250cc single was probably overkill! Generally it seemed that the brake would work if correctly set up, but could not dissipate heat efficiently enough to avoid fade in heavy, prolonged use. Interestingly, the swept area of this brake was approximately 10 per cent less than the previous Triumph 8in-diameter TLS brake, which helps to explain its inferior performance.

The design of the brake was good in parts. It did away with the complex and difficult to set up mechanical linkage seen on the previous TLS brake, and used the cable to operate both brake arms. The cable outer was mounted on one brake arm, and the end of the cable was fixed on the second arm. The theory was that this would provide equal, self-adjusting pressure on both leading shoes, resulting in a brake that was, in effect, always providing the same amount of braking from both shoes. Interestingly BMW used an identical method of operating its TLS brake on the R69S in the 1950s and 1960s. Individual adjustment of the two brake shoe pivots was provided for using a standard automotive 'click-stop' mechanism, enabling easy and precise setting up of the brake. The brake design overcame the problem of balancing the shoes on a TLS brake where the

The conical hubs used from 1971 looked good, but the front brake did not perform as well as the previous twin leader.

brake cams are operated by a rod connecting a single lever pulled by a cable to the second lever. Anyone who has tried to set up the previous BSA/Triumph TLS brake will know that this is a fiddly job needing at least three hands to do it properly, and if not done correctly will seriously compromise the performance of the brake.

As good as this aspect of the design was, however, it was overshadowed by a fundamental problem in the operating mechanism. A Bowden cable is designed to guide an inner cable from one fixed point (the handlebar lever) to another (the cable stop on the brake plate) – the outer should act only as a guide. However, the new BSA design relied on the cable to both guide the inner cable and act as an end stop. A Bowden cable outer is essentially a close-wound spring, and can compress and reduce in length. This is not a problem in a conventional brake where the cable outer is simply guiding the cable from the lever to the brake, because the outer is subject to little (if any) compressive force as the cable inner is pulling between and against two fixed points. In the Umberslade brake, pulling on the brake-lever presses the brake shoes against the brake drum, but will also compress the outer cable, reducing the force available to be converted into braking. Triumph did appear to have taken this effect into account by providing a large-diameter cable, much more robust than any that had been used previously. Despite this, in normal use, correctly set up and using the heavyweight cable, the Triumph brake is pretty good, although it could suffer from fade when used heavily. The use of non-standard cables can result in much diminished efficiency, as a disproportionate amount of the force exerted by the rider's hand on the brake lever is used to compress the outer cable.

Contemporary road tests show reasonable stopping distances from 30mph (48km/h), but identified that heavy use led to the brake fading, despite the large air scoop on the front of the brake-plate. A secondary problem was water ingress. If a bike was left on its side stand,

rainwater collected in the brake because of inadequate sealing. This resulted in some interesting braking characteristics as the brake goes from not working at all when drenched through to excessive 'grabbiness' at low speeds as it begins to dry out – exactly what you don't want a brake to do when the roads are wet. The problem is that the brake backplate is on the opposite side to the side stand; this results in leaning the bike over, such that water will get into the brake but won't drain out while the bike is standing, which gives the shoes a good soaking. If the brake is properly set up it is no worse than many contemporary drum brakes, but the ultimate solution is the fitting of a disc brake from a later 650 or 750 Triumph.

Why Triumph spent so much time and effort in producing a new drum brake when they should have been developing a disc is lost in the mists of time – especially as they introduced a disc brake in late 1972.

For 1973 the 750cc bikes received a Lockheed disc brake at the front. The unit worked well and remained unchanged until the demise of the Meriden-built twins.

The Triumph disc brake was first introduced on the 750cc Trident in the 1973 season and was fitted as standard to the 750cc twins, both the T140V Bonneville and TR7RV Tiger, when they appeared in September 1973. The 650cc twins were destined not to have the disc brake fitted as standard until the following model year (1974), when the disc-braked five-speed T120V was the only 650cc model in the range (the TR6R Tiger and TR6C Trophy models had been dropped by then). The brake was developed jointly by Triumph and Lockheed, and featured a 10in (254mm) diameter hard chrome-plated cast iron disc bolted to a new front wheel hub, which was gripped by a hydraulically operated, twin opposed-cylinder calliper mounted on the drive-side fork slider. The brake was operated from a new handlebar lever, with the master cylinder and fluid reservoir fixed to the back of the existing Lucas handlebar switch-gear. A screw-on top with rubber gasket sealed the fluid reservoir, and a chromed steel lever operated the brake. The clutch lever was also chromed steel, signalling the end of the high quality forged alloy levers previously fitted. The brake was well received and it worked well even in the wet, when most Japanese discs of the time suffered from wet lag. The hard chrome soon wore off, exposing the cast iron of the rotor to the elements and promoting rust, but this was considered an acceptable price to pay for a brake that worked well in all conditions. Twin front discs were fitted as standard to the TSS and were offered as an option on the other bikes in the range in 1982.

Legislation in the USA dictated a left-foot gear change, and this meant that the Co-op took the opportunity for 1976 to standardize on brakes by fitting a similar Lockheed disc to the rear. A new foot pedal connected to a master cylinder positioned awkwardly behind the lower frame member, where it could collect road dirt and water. The hydraulic fluid reservoir was placed under the seat, connected to the master cylinder by a long hose. A brand new

rear hub carried the rear-brake disc rotor, which was slightly thinner than the previous year's front unit, and this specification of disc was standardized for both front and rear. The calliper was slung underneath the swinging arm, and, like the master cylinder, was badly exposed to road dirt and rain. However, the brake did work well and when introduced the Triumphs were the only bikes on the market with a disc at the rear – a good marketing point that was exploited by Triumph at the time.

The rear disc's master cylinder was badly positioned behind the rear engine plate, where it was both difficult to access and exposed to road dirt. Its fluid reservoir was fitted under the seat and was connected to the master cylinder by a tube. One problem with the new disc brake was that the increased braking power and new hub design meant that the rear spokes were prone to snapping. This was cured with the T140E by increasing the spoke gauge. The calliper was eventually moved above the swinging arm, initially only on the T140D for 1979, but was also fitted to the other models in the range for 1980. The 1983 TSX 'Custom' model had a new Italian Brembo rear-brake master cylinder repositioned on the rear footrest carrier, where it was out of the way of road dirt and debris. This unit had its reservoir built in so it was no longer placed under the seat.

The Thunderbird and Tiger Trail were fitted with the standard single front disc, but the rear featured a rod-operated 7in (178mm) diameter drum brake. The brake drum bolted onto a modified hub, and the brake plate assembly was very closely related to the unit fitted to the conical hub models.

The Harris Bonneville retained the disc brakes, but because of supply problems had to source them from Italy. The bikes had twin 10¼in (260mm) diameter front disc brakes, with twin opposed-piston Italian Brembo callipers, and a single disc, again with Brembo callipers, at the rear. Brembo supplied the master cylinders, with the front unit handlebar mounted as

The T140 rear disc was operated from the right-hand side. The master cylinder was positioned inboard of the footrest hanger, where it was exposed to spray and road dirt.

before, while the rear was positioned higher up on the rear sub-frame, in a similar position to that used on the final TSX model, where it was not so susceptible to road spray.

Electrics

At the introduction of the unit 650s and through to the end of the range with the 750s, a Lucas AC alternator supplied the electrical power. Initially all bikes in the range were 6 volt. The bikes came equipped with the bare minimum of electrical fittings: coil ignition, 6 volt battery and rectifier, 7in (178mm) diameter chromed headlamp (6in/152mm on the TR6) with dip, main and pilot (or parking) lights, a rear stop and tail light and a horn. A simple, cheap chromed steel handlebar switch operated the dip/main and horn on the 6T and T120, while the TR6 had a push-button horn switch on the handlebars with the dip/main-beam functions operated from a push-button inconveniently positioned in the headlamp shell. A major problem with the 6 volt system was that it was in effect unregulated, with the power supply depending on switching in extra alternator coils for ignition, pilot light and full lighting. The system was not the most reliable, depending heavily on the operation of the fiendishly complicated Lucas combined light and ignition switch to provide the correct amount of charge to the battery. The situation persisted until 1965, when the Thunderbird's electrics were changed to 12 volts. The standard Lucas 12 volt system used had a solid-state zener diode fitted to regulate the battery voltage: the diode would go 'open circuit' when the battery was fully charged around 13/14 volts and would take the excess output of the alternator by converting it to heat, thus providing active control of the battery charge. The Thunderbird featured a large flat alloy plate under the fuel tank to act as a heat sink. This worked well, as it was positioned in the air stream.

The Thunderbird was the first of the unit 650s to get 12 volt electrics. The zener diode handled voltage regulation and was mounted on a large heat sink.

The rest of the range gained 12 volt electrics the following year (1966), but the reliability of the system was compromised by moving the heat sink to a position under the left-hand side panel, where the zener could overheat and burn out. With a new finned bullet-shaped heat sink mounted under the headlamp for 1968, the electrical system was pretty much bulletproof.

While the Thunderbird retained the traditional Triumph nacelle, which carried a combined light and ignition switch and ammeter, the TR6 and T120 had bullet-shaped chromed headlamps, suspended between two 'ears' fitted between the top and bottom fork yokes. The ammeter was fitted in the headlamp shell. The TR6 and T120 ignition and light switches were rotary units and started life on the left-hand side panel. For 1967, warning lights were fitted in the headlamp shell: green for ignition on and red for main beam. The light switch also moved to the headlamp shell in 1967. The rotary light switch was replaced with a toggle switch in 1968, and the same year saw the ignition switch moved to the headlamp mounting ear, a much more convenient place where it was easily accessible by the rider. A warning light for oil pressure was fitted for 1969, along with a new Lucas RM21 encapsulated stator alternator and a front brake-light switch, which was operated by a pressure switch in the front-brake cable.

The US specification TR6C had a 6in (152mm) headlamp with a black painted body. When lights were fitted, this carried two push toggle switches for on/off and dip/main.

With the introduction of the oil-in-frame models in 1971, the electrical system was updated and modernized, primarily by having direction indicators fitted as standard. The headlamp was a flat-backed design, with an offset rotary light switch (parking/main) on its top and three coloured warning lights (orange for indicators, red for oil pressure, blue for main beam) on the back edge, and a large rubber cover at the back concealing the wires. It was carried on rubber-mounted wire brackets, with the standard front indicator stems used to fix the headlamp to the brackets. The indicators were chromed plastic bullet-shaped Lucas units and the round amber lenses were the same as used on Land Rovers at the time. The rear light was the standard Lucas 679 'tit' type, and this was carried on a pressed steel unit that placed the light behind the line of the rear mudguard as required by US legislation. The indicators were bolted to the side of the unit and the whole assembly was unkindly nicknamed 'the Gargoyle', as it resembled the protuberances seen on medieval cathedrals.

The handlebar switches were, at last, tasteful cast-aluminium units. Each unit was the same in appearance and comprised alloy castings with the handlebar lever pivots on the front and a standardized switch console on the rear (facing the rider). Each console had a central toggle switch with either two positions for dip/main or three positions for the indicators. In addition there were two press-and-hold buttons above and below the toggle switch.

For 1971 the right-hand switch toggle operated the indicators, with the toggle being operated up for left and down for right, and the top press-button operated the ignition kill function. The left-hand cluster's toggle operated the dip/main beam, with the lower push-button operating the horn and the upper operating the headlamp flasher. The bikes lost the ammeter at this time, and the new handlebar switches came in for some criticism, being not as easy to use as equivalent Japanese units.

The ignition switch was fitted in the rear of the right-hand side panel and was a four-position unit: parking lights only, everything off, ignition on, and ignition and lights on. The switch was awkward to reach and the key could be broken off when a rider or pillion passenger got on or off the bike.

The introduction of the 750cc T140V and TR7RV in 1973 resulted in some changes to the electrical equipment. The big square Lucas L917 light, with built-in side reflectors and mounted on an alloy housing, replaced the L679 Gargoyle unit, and the ignition switch was also moved

back to the left-hand-side headlamp ear, which was rubber-mounted to give some isolation from vibration for the headlamp. The headlamp shell reverted to the traditional chromed bullet-shaped item, with three warning lights and the toggle light switch positioned in its back, along with two black stick-on decals to annotate the light and switch functions in line with US legislation. The introduction of the 750cc models also saw a new ergonomically designed left-hand-side handlebar switch, which operated the dip/main, indicators, horn and headlamp flasher. To comply with legislation, the unit had the switch functions cast into the casing. The right-hand switch was now the previous indicator switch wired to act as a toggle kill switch, giving off/on/off. The two push-buttons were not wired up, and the toggle itself

The T140V had decent handlebar switches that were almost as good as the Japanese opposition. Instruments were rubber mounted in separate pods. Note the NVT 'Wiggly Worm' logo on this 1977 example.

was now extended and moulded in red plastic, and a sticker showed the switch functions.

This layout continued until the T140E range was introduced for 1979. These bikes featured a negative earth electrical system, with a more powerful 180 watt three-phase alternator and twin zener diode charge control. This meant that the electrical system could handle the soon to be announced electric start. New black-painted cast alloy handlebar switches were introduced, which incorporated integral alloy levers, at last banishing the cheap-looking chromed steel levers. The handlebar switches were similar to those fitted to the Norton Commando Mk III, with the left-hand unit in effect a re-housed version of the previous unit with dip/main beam, horn, headlamp flasher and indicators, and the right-hand unit operating the kill switch, the headlight/pilot light and the starter (when fitted). The warning lights and ignition switch were mounted in a centre console between the instruments and was the same unit as fitted to the T160 Trident. There were now four warning lights: oil pressure (red), indicators (yellow), main beam (blue) and neutral (green). The only change to this layout came with the first year TR65 Thunderbird and Tiger Trail, when the centre console was deleted and the warning lights and ignition switch were incorporated into the empty tachometer binnacle, a cost-cutting move that looked cheap and was not appreciated by the buyers.

Instruments

The bikes from 1963 to 1970 were equipped with a speedometer and headlamp-mounted ammeter, and an optional tachometer. On their introduction the bikes were equipped with Smiths chronometric instruments, but these were quickly superseded in 1964 by Smiths magnetic-type instruments, which were cheaper than the chronometric, but not as reliable or as accurate. An indication of the superior quality of the chronometric instruments was their use

on police bikes up until the 1970s. The police bike instruments had to be specially calibrated to enable a speed reading to be admissible in court and the magnetic instruments simply could not supply the required level of accuracy.

When fitted, the paired speedometer and tachometer on the pre oil-in-frame models were mounted on a rubber-mounted bracket, which was bolted to the fork top yoke via two metalastic bushes, giving the instruments some insulation from vibration. Models such as the TR6, which did not have a tachometer as standard, had a single instrument bracket, which was not rubber-mounted, while the 6T Thunderbird had the speedometer mounted in the nacelle.

For 1964, the bikes were equipped with Smiths grey-faced instruments, with the speedometer reading clockwise and the tachometer (Smiths type RSM 3001/02), when fitted, reading anticlockwise as a result of the direct drive from the end of the exhaust camshaft. The speedo read from 0 to 120mph (Smiths type SSM 5001/00 on the TR6 and T120, and SSM 5001/00 on the 6T) and was equipped with the standard five-digit milometer (0 to 99,999 miles) and a resettable trip function that read up to 999.9 miles. Note that, as standard, the 6T was never fitted with a tachometer. For 1966 the tachometer (RSM 3003/01) was changed to clockwise rotation following the introduction of the new 90-degree tachometer drive gearbox. In 1967 the speedometer was upgraded to read from 0 to 150mph (Type SSM 5001/06), and in late 1970 both the speedo and tachometer gained black faces (SSM 5007/00, tachometer RSM 3003/13).

One aside was the fitting of speedometers manufactured by German firm VDO as an option for the 1966, 1967 and 1968 TR6C models. The 'VDO Enduro Speedo' was the subject of a Triumph Corporation Service Bulletin, dated 22 February 1965, which gave instructions on how to use a mounting bracket kit (part number CD433) to fit the instrument.

The 1960s Bonneville and Trophy models had their speedo and (when fitted) tachometer mounted on a plate that was rubber mounted on the top yoke. This 1968 Trophy has the standard Smiths grey-faced instruments.

The speedo was the same diameter as the original equipment Smiths unit, but its body was much deeper than the Smiths' magnetic type. The VDO speedo also had a trip meter with the reset knob placed on the face of the instrument, making it easier to get at than the Smiths side-mounted version.

The 1971 oil-in-frame models had the same black-faced Smiths magnetic-type speedometer and tachometers fitted as standard as were on the late 1970 models, but lost the ammeter. They were mounted in separate rubber cups, which were in turn mounted on separate 'figure of eight'-shaped chromed steel brackets that fitted under the stanchion fork top nuts.

The black-faced Smiths instruments had the NVT 'Wiggly Worm' logo added to them for the 1975 model year, but the logo was discontinued during 1977 for the 1978 models: the 1977 brochure shows the bike equipped with the branded instruments. Supply difficulties with Smiths clocks led to the introduction of alternative Veglia instruments, with white figures and needles on a black face, during the 1978 production run on some bikes. The Veglia instruments were standardized for the 1979 model year, when the foreign instruments were marked 'Meriden' on their faces.

This branding only lasted for the 1979 model year, which also saw the introduction of the

*The T140E had new rubber binnacles to carry the Veglia instruments that were fitted from 1979.
The first batches of these instruments were branded 'Meriden', as seen on the speedo here. Also note the
T140E-style handlebar switches and the choke lever, which at last has been moved back onto the handlebars.*

Triumph T160 Trident-style instrument console, which had a triangular-shaped instrument panel fitted between the instruments. These were now rubber-mounted in new alloy binnacles. The Les Harris bikes continued with this layout.

Note that the 1982 Thunderbird was equipped with only a speedometer and had its ignition switch and warning lights fitted in the tachometer binnacle.

Conclusion

The longevity of the Triumph-twin design is a tribute to Edward Turner, who, despite his faults, laid down a fundamentally 'right' design in 1938 that lasted the test of time and remained in production for some fifty years. Never mind that one of the few common components between a 1938 Speed Twin and a 1988 Harris Bonneville is the oil pump drive block (part number E495/70-0495) – the genetics of the design are the same and even the appearance is not that much different. If you take a 1963 model and compare it to the last 1980s models then the similarities are even more marked and it is still easy to see the 'bloodline' of the bike running from one to another. This is one of the Triumph 'B' series's fundamental charms: its connection to its own past and heritage, something that no other modern marque, except perhaps Morgan cars, can claim.

8 BSA A65 Engine Versus Triumph 650

The Triumph unit-650 engine was introduced in 1962 (for the 1963 season). This was the same year that BSA, Triumph's partner and rival, introduced its unit 500cc and 650cc engines, the A50 and A65. A simple analysis of both engine designs shows the interesting fact that the BSA A65 motor had a number of advantages over the Triumph unit-650 in design terms, but only one disadvantage. The following analysis appeared in the author's first book, *BSA Unit-Construction Twins* (The Crowood Press, 2004), but is reproduced in a modified form as it is very relevant to the Triumph 'B' Series twins.

Looking first at the top end, the A65 had almost square cylinder dimensions (bore/stroke of 75 × 74mm), which enabled it to have a much more efficient cylinder head/combustion chamber design when compared to the Triumph. The Triumph B Series twin with its bore and stroke of 71 × 82mm had, relative to the

The A65 and Bonneville were different interpretations of the same specification for a sports 650cc twin. The Triumph kept its pre-unit looks, while the BSA 'water melon' engine was streamlined and sleek.

BSA, a long stroke, which theoretically resulted in less room for big valves in the cylinder head and hence less efficient breathing and higher piston speeds. Despite this apparent advantage, the valve sizes in the BSA were very similar to those in the relevant Triumph: a 1970 BSA Lightning had inlet and exhaust valve diameters of 1.60in and 1.41in, while the equivalent 1970 T120 Bonneville measured 1.59in and 1.44in.

An additional advantage that the BSA had over the Triumph was that, owing to the longer stroke, Triumph piston speeds were higher than those in the BSA at given revs. This meant that the Triumph's safe maximum rev limit was lower than the BSA's. This was reflected in the road test data of the time. Contemporary 1971 US road tests had a BSA Lightning claiming 52bhp at 7,000rpm, and the 1971 Triumph T120R claiming 48bhp at 6,700rpm, both bikes having 9:1 compression ratios. Attempts to verify these figures from factory sources uncovered an interesting detail. The 1970 Triumph workshop manual gives a power output of 47bhp, while the 1970 USA Triumph owners' handbook says 50bhp (with straight-through exhaust pipes).

The BSA A65 top end also had a well thought-out layout. BSA engineers took the opportunity to eliminate the need to carry the rocker shafts in separate rocker boxes, unlike both the previous BSA A10 and the Triumph. The BSA's rocker shafts were carried directly in trunnions cast into the head and proved to be an accurate and rigid assembly. The lack of

The A65 engine retained the layout of its pre-unit ancestor, but was given a styling makeover. The engine's shape was not to everyone's liking, but it looked more modern than the Triumph unit.

The A65 had its rocker shafts carried in cast-in mounts in the head. This meant the rocker cover was unstressed and allowed excellent access to adjust the tappets.

separate rocker box or boxes also meant that all of the A50/A65 cylinder-head bolts were bolted directly through the head into the barrel, making it easy to achieve accurate torque figures on these most vital of fasteners.

In contrast, on the Triumph unit-650 engine, four out of the nine head bolts were used to hold down the rocker boxes as well as the head, leading to a less than straightforward procedure to achieve a suitable torque figure for all head bolts. This feature was compounded by the compressibility of the composite gaskets required between the rocker boxes and the head. This problem has only recently been partially solved with the introduction of solid copper rocker-box gaskets for the Triumph twin engine. Two further advantages of the BSA system were that the rocker cover enclosed the whole top of the head and was unstressed, making it easy to achieve an oil-tight seal when it was on, and with the cover off you could see all four valves, rockers and adjusters, making it easier to carry out adjustments. This is in stark contrast to the Triumph with its poor access to the tappet adjusters, and the loss-prone round individual tappet covers.

A final benefit of the BSA's head design was the easy refitting of pushrods to the rockers, again in stark contrast to Triumph's fiddly task of blindly locating both ends of the pushrods before bolting down the rocker box.

Moving down from the cylinder head, the BSA top half had the pushrod tunnel cast into the barrels. In a stroke, this eliminated another problem area with which Triumph owners are all too familiar, stopping oil leaks from the individual inlet and exhaust pushrod tubes. The problems a Triumph has with these are illustrated by the virtually yearly changes to these components and their assorted sealing mechanisms – changes that never really solved the problem.

Overall the top end of the BSA was a much more elegant design than the 650 Triumph, both in terms of production engineering, where it was easier to assemble at the factory and had fewer parts, and ease of use for the owner in terms of tappet adjustment and the ease of torquing down the head bolts and nuts. It had fewer parts than the Triumph, was easier to dismantle and reassemble, had fewer points that oil could leak from, and did not have anywhere near the same potential to loose tappet covers!

It was a shame that the Triumph designers never managed to solve the same problems in some twenty years of production of the unit 650 and 750 engines. For all its advantages in its design and layout, however, the BSA top end design had to concede some advantages to the Triumph engine. With its high-mounted fore and aft twin camshafts, the Triumph design had short and light pushrods, which were more rigid and lighter than the BSA design. In addition, the rockers themselves were more compact and, again, lighter and more rigid than the BSA's. All this led to a very efficient set of valve gear, which, despite the theoretical advantages of the BSA design, allowed the Triumph to rev better than the BSA. These factors tended to overcome

The A65 had a single, gear-driven camshaft positioned behind the crank. This meant better cooling for the barrel and also featured a pushrod tunnel that was cast into the barrel, a more oil-tight solution than Triumph's leaky pushrod tubes.

the disadvantages of the Triumph's top end, and gave the Triumph engine its 'tunability' that led to the Triumph engine outgunning the BSA unit on both the road and track.

The bottom end of the BSA engine had some advantages over the Triumph, and one major disadvantage. In the BSA engine, the layout of the single camshaft and the primary-chain tensioner were both much better than those of the Triumph. The BSA has a single, gear-driven camshaft situated behind the barrels, as opposed to the Triumph's two gear-driven camshafts, front and rear of the barrels. The BSA system has fewer parts and less frictional losses. This makes for an elegant design that uses the minimum number of parts combined with good engineering practice. The application of these principles led to a system that needed virtually no maintenance, but the Triumph design, with its twin high-mounted camshafts, enabled a light and rigid drive to the valve gear.

The BSA primary-chain tensioner was much more sensible than that fitted to the Triumph. The BSA had a silicon rubber-faced pivoted blade, controlled by a bolt screwed vertically into the bottom of the primary chain case, while the Triumph had a sprung steel blade controlled by a long shaft joining the two ends of the blade together.

The BSA tensioner hinged on a rod that was rigidly supported at both ends, one in the left-hand-side crankcase, and the other in the primary-chain case. The whole chain-adjusting operation was much easier and more straightforward than the Triumph's blade-type tensioner. Accessibility to the BSA tensioner mechanism was easy, unlike the Triumph, where the lower frame cradle obscured the adjuster hole, and adjustment could be carried out using a normal spanner. The operation was intuitive: screw in the tensioner to increase tension, out to decrease. The Triumph mechanism required a special tool, mainly because of the difficult access, and the feel of the mechanism was much more imprecise than the BSA, making it difficult to gauge if the tension of the chain was correct. In addition the BSA mechanism was robust in comparison with the Triumph, which has the real potential for the tensioner blade to break if overtightened.

The major disadvantage of the BSA engine's bottom half was the perception that it had a weak bottom end. There is no doubt that there was a problem, but why there was a problem is open to debate. The bottom end of the BSA engine had plain big-end bearings and two main bearings; the drive side was originally a ball race (replaced with a lipped roller in 1966) and the timing side a plain bush. Oil was fed under pressure to the big ends through the timing-side bush. Filtration was minimal, with wire mesh filters in the sump and oil tank. As was standard practice at the time, a sludge trap was incorporated in the crank, which acted as a centrifugal filter to catch any solids before they reached the big ends.

While the early BSA motors were reliable, however, problems started to appear as the design aged. Power output was increased throughout the 1960s, going from a claimed 38bhp from the 1963 A65 Star to a claimed 55bhp from the 1966 Spitfire Mk II. This increase was achieved through progressive development of the engine. While the bikes' performance increased dramatically, the downside of this increase in power was increased stress on the engine, leading to increased wear on components. The problem was exacerbated with the introduction of the lipped roller main bearing on the drive side in 1966, which was more sensitive to the crank location and end float.

While Triumph and other manufacturers suffered from the same equation of ever-increasing power with little fundamental reworking of the basic designs, on the A50 and A65 engines there was a critical design factor that could lead to disaster. Once the plain timing-side bush had some wear in it, the oil pressure and oil volume fed to the big ends would progressively reduce, and as engine revolutions increased, oil pressure

at the drive-side big end would be inadequate to handle the load, eventually leading to the drive-side big end failing.

Another source of carnage in the BSA design was the effectiveness of the timing-side main bush location. Inadequate location of the bush in the crankcases, coupled with excessive end float on the crank, could result in the bush turning in the cases. The oil feed to the timing-side bearing came through an oilway in the crankcases into a hole in the outer bush. The oil lubricates the bearing and then proceeds (against centripetal force) via a radius drilling in the crankshaft to the big ends. Turning of the bearing outer resulted in the oil supply being cut off to the main bearing – and the big ends – with catastrophic results.

The A65 primary drive used a triplex chain against the 650 Triumph's duplex, and featured a neat slipper chain tensioner, which was much easier to adjust than the Triumph's.

The A65 engine is a bit bland when compared to the Triumph.

Basically, it has to be said that the A65 bottom end could not cope with as much abuse as the Triumph twin engine could: the unit 650 Triumph bottom end had ball and roller mains, with oil fed directly to the plain big ends from the end of the crankshaft. If a Triumph was running its main bearings, it tended to give plenty of warning through noise and vibration, but the big-end oil supply tended not to be affected. In fact, in this state the Triumph engine was considered to give its best performance – the fact that Triumph engines usually run best just before they blow up seemed to be the maxim of Triumph tuners in the late 1960s and is still recognized today. Looking at the Triumph's engine design this is probably correct!

Essentially, once an A50/65 timing-side bush was worn, then the engine was on notice of impending disaster. The first serious symptom would be a main-bearing rumble and increased vibration, followed by a big-end knock. If ignored, these symptoms would result in a seized big end (usually the drive side) or a broken drive-side conrod, the severity of the damage tending to increase with the number of revs being used at the time. However, there are records of well-maintained A65s (those having regular oil changes) lasting for comparable numbers of miles as the equivalent Triumph, although this does not take into account the differences between riders! I suspect that in a controlled test the Triumph engine would last longer than the BSA, as the bottom end is better able to resist wear and abuse without suffering a catastrophic failure. The engines are indeed pretty well matched, which is not that surprising when you consider that they were designed by the best brains in the British industry at the time.

9 Owning and Riding

Any of the Triumph twins covered in this book can provide reliable and enjoyable riding in modern traffic, with good performance, stamina, handling and brakes. However, there are a number of modifications to increase performance and 'usability', often based on what the factory did, that can improve the bikes and their owners' experiences. When carrying out improvements there can be issues over originality, but in the case of the Triumph 'B' series bikes there are lots of original specification machines in existence and, since they are probably the most numerous of the British classics, I do not think that it is an issue to carry out

modifications. In fact, in its final years the factory would build just about anything that a customer wanted! Owners can use later components (the TLS brakes fitted from 1968 spring to mind here) or aftermarket accessories (Boyer electronic ignition is a good example) to build for themselves the bike that they really want – and not fear altering an original classic.

The raison d'être of the Triumph Twin was to offer the British biking experience to the widest possible market, and indeed it probably remains the most practical machine available to do this. There are lots of good quality spares still being made, all the bikes in the range have

There are lots of non-standard Triumph Twins about. Here, an early oil-in-frame model has had a flat-track style overhaul.

the performance to make them capable of keeping up with modern traffic, they are fundamentally reliable, there are lots of them around and they are sensibly priced. The popularity of the model means that there is plenty of mechanical expertise available and there are no real issues that a competent amateur mechanic cannot overcome with a bit of application. And finally the bikes look so good.

Maintenance and Improvements

Engine Improvements for Reliability

The engine on the 650s and 750s is pretty reliable. To keep it that way, probably the best modification is to fit a full-flow oil filter in the return feed to the oil tank, thus, it is to be hoped, keeping the oil clean. The filter will also increase the amount of oil in circulation, which is especially beneficial for the oil-in-frame models with their marginal oil capacity.

A second thing to do is to change the oil regularly: for the 650s and 750s Triumph recommended changing the oil every 1,500 miles (2,400km), and this should be adhered to today. Modify the oil change routine so that it is every 1,500 miles or yearly, whichever comes first. If you are replacing the oil pump it is worth fitting the late Type 4 valve oil pump to almost guarantee that oil pressure will be maintained even

A full-flow oil filter can be fitted unobtrusively behind the engine cases on the T120 and the T140. Here is a neat installation on a T140.

if there are impurities present in the oil. Some people recommend a Morgo-type rotary pump, which delivers a constant flow of oil (as opposed to the Triumph plunger pump, which gives pulses of pressure) and can give a higher pressure and flow rate, but these are probably not needed for everyday use. It is a good idea to fit a new oil-pressure release valve. This is housed in the large domed nut on the timing side of the engine and contains a spring-loaded valve designed to bleed oil off at a set pressure. The spring will lose tension over the years and so your valve may well be lowering your oil pressure to the big ends to an unacceptable level. Finally an oil cooler is a useful addition, especially for the oil-in-frame models, which can run hot; these not only help the engine run cooler but also increase the oil capacity by a pint or so.

If you are rebuilding the engine, make sure that you clean out the sludge trap in the crank. This is a centrifugal oil filter and it will fill up with solidified sludge over time. If it is left, it will eventually fill up the crankshaft oil gallery and cut off the oil supply to the big ends, with catastrophic results. Do not undo the sludge trap plug with an impact driver, as this can stress the crankshaft, and replace it with one that can be tightened with an Allen key; these are much easier to undo when the time for the next rebuild arrives. Make sure there are no nicks or scratches on the conrods, as these can cause stress points resulting in breakage. Weigh the pistons and conrods and take material off the insides of the pistons to make them weigh the same, and then have the whole crank dynamically balanced. This will help to make the engine smoother, and a smooth-running engine will last longer. Other hints and tips on engine tuning and rebuilding can be found in Stan Shenton's *Triumph Tuning*.

One final modification is to the tappet adjusters. There are two types available, the 'mushroom' type, with a ball bearing on the valve end for precise alignment, and those with an ordinary flat base but with an Allen key

Modifications do not have to be obtrusive. The Norman Hyde oil cooler fitted to Nick Vale's T140V nestles between the frame's front down-tubes.

Mikuni carburettors can be fitted to the Triumph twin. Modified inlet stubs allow for rubber mounting.

adjustment, rather than raised flats as on the standard type. The Allen key adjustment makes it easy to set up the tappet clearance, while the 'mushroom' type gives more even wear on the valve tip and a better 'push', which lessens guide wear as there are reduced sideways forces on the valve. The only downside is that you need to be careful when tightening them after adjustment as they can break, since their shafts are hollow to allow the hexagon for the Allen key.

Carburettors

The Amal Monobloc carburettor is generally considered to be a robust and reliable instrument. Other than giving them a good overhaul and clean there is not much wrong with them. New replacements are available, as are most spare parts. Its replacement, the Amal Concentric Mk1, is not so well regarded. The Concentric was designed to be cheaper to produce than the Monobloc, and despite its simple design actually works very well. However, it wears quickly, leading to air leaks around the slide, which play havoc with a reliable tick-over. The body can also distort if the fixing flange nuts are over-tightened, which results in a sticking slide. The use of a hard chromed slide reduces wear to the carburettor body, and it is always worthwhile to use an air filter to help to cut down wear on both the carburettor and the engine. New complete carburettors are available, as are all parts. Finally the Concentric is prone to blockages in the pilot air passages that are difficult to clear. This is a particular problem with carburettors that have been left standing with petrol in them for a while, and the only way to clean them out is using an ultrasonic cleaner – poking wires down the passages will distort the carefully sized jets and should be not be encouraged!

The Concentric Mk2 seems to work well, and the main problem seems to be wear in the choke mechanism, leading to rich running. (Replacement Mk2s and spares were hard to come by at the time of writing.)

The final solution is to replace the Amal instrument with a suitable Mikuni unit. While this fix is not original and needs special fixings and air filter arrangements, users say they give a more reliable tick-over and retain their tune better than their Amal equivalents. Cost is about the same as getting a new Amal Concentric Mk1.

Primary Drive and Gearbox

There is not a lot wrong with the clutch or primary drive. Companies such as SRM produce alloy clutch pressure plates, which are lighter and more rigid than the pressed steel standard units, and also have mushroom-headed clutch pressure plate lifters with needle roller bearings giving smoother operation and less wear than the standard items. Various suppliers offer uprated clutch components such as springs and plates, and belt-drive conversions, which are said to result in smoother power delivery and less vibration.

Electrical Improvements

As with the engine, the later 12 volt electrical system is pretty reliable. If you have a 6 volt system then the best thing to do from a performance point of view is to convert it to 12 volts. If you don't want to go down that route, preferring to keep the bike original, then make sure that any electrical losses in the system are minimized. This means cleaning and protecting all connections and switches, and running new earth wires where needed. There are more powerful 6 volt bulbs available now from various suppliers that will improve lighting. Also

make sure your headlamp reflector is in tip-top condition: if so, the 'candle in the brown beer bottle' scenario should not occur!

Whether you stick with 6 volts or change to 12 volts, it is a good idea to get a new encapsulated alternator stator. An unencapsulated original will be at least forty years old and can fail at any time, as I recently found out for myself. The rotor should be fine if the centre is still firmly attached to the body and it can support its own weight if you lift it up with a spanner – but check all the magnets around its periphery and not just one.

If your bike has the zener diode hidden behind the side panel, then buy a proper heat sink and fit it under the headlamp where it will keep cool. The old-style silicon plate rectifiers are easily damaged and can be replaced by the small, cheap square box type, which is reliable and has less power loss than the older ones.

A number of suppliers, including Sparx, Boyer and Podtronics, produce solid-state combined regulator and rectifiers. These black boxes are connected to the alternator and output regulated 12 volt DC. They can be slotted into the standard wiring loom, replacing the rectifier and the zener diode, and provide reliable battery charging. Sparx even produces a neat regulator and rectifier unit that replaces the bullet-shaped zener diode unit under the headlamp: it looks original and fits directly in place of the zener heat sink.

Finally, with all the new charging components you can fit an H4 headlamp so you can see where you are going at night and other drivers can see you. The standard system will handle a 60W headlamp: my T120 has one fitted and the battery stays fully charged, with a new stator, zener diode and square-type rectifier. I have found the Wipac 'Quadoptic' unit fits and is resistant to the vertical-twin vibration.

Ignition System

If you want to avoid using electronic ignition, the early 4CA Lucas points should be replaced with the later 6CA units to enable accurate timing of both cylinders. The mechanical advance retard unit should be carefully inspected and if it shows any signs of wear it should be replaced – and the likelihood is that it will be worn out. The ultimate fix for the ignition system is to fit an electronic system. There are several systems on the market. Among these I have used Boyer and Sparx systems, both of which work well, are 'fit and forget' and are reliable. I've run a Boyer on my T120 for ten years and have had no problems other than ones of my own making (*see* section below). I have also run a Sparx electronic ignition system, which is almost identical to the Boyer, on a T100C for three years, again with no problems. Note that, while the T140Es and TR7RV Tigers had the Lucas Rita system fitted as standard from 1979, the later Thunderbird did not.

Boyer electronic ignition is a bolt-on modification, replacing the points backplate and advance retard unit. This is unobtrusive and it is easy to return the bike to points if required.

If you fit electronic ignition it is worth fitting new coils. Both Sparx and Boyer need 6 volt coils wired in series as they operate on the 'spare spark' principle. In any case, I would recommend replacing all ignition components on any rebuilt bike if you are not sure of the provenance of the system (original coils and condensers could be forty-five years old). Finally, don't forget the ignition switch and the kill switch. These can also be pretty old, so make sure they are working well as faults in them can give rise to all sorts of strange misfires or ignition failures.

Chassis and Braking

The chassis used on the 650 and 750cc twins are both good. Although the later pre oil-in-frame chassis is better than the earlier ones, in normal road use the early frames are perfectly adequate. New swinging-arm bushes and taper roller head bearings will make a difference, and the later 'shuttle valve' forks also perform better than the earlier versions. The main improvement that can be easily made to the early bikes is the fitting of a TLS front brake. This is not cheap as it will need the appropriate flanged hub and the correct wide fork yokes, but it does give excellent braking that is up to today's crowded traffic conditions.

There are few improvements I would recommend for the oil-in-frame bikes. The handling and roadholding of the frame is excellent, and the front forks are also very good. The conical hub TLS brake can be replaced with a disc front end, which can be uprated to twin discs, either using a late fork slider from an existing twin-disc setup or by using an early disc slider and turning it through 180 degrees so the calliper is forward of the fork leg.

True Twin Tales

I currently own a 1970 T120R, but back in the mid-1980s I also owned a 1979 T140E. The experiences of owning these bikes, and the stories of other owners and riders, provide a good picture of what it was like to own one of these bikes when they were fairly new, and what they are like to own and ride today.

Pete Isted's 1968 Bonneville, 1970s

One trip I took with Pete Isted on his 1968 Triumph Bonneville has stuck in my memory. The trip was our yearly pilgrimage to South Wales from the our homes in north Hampshire in search of sun (well, drizzle), sea and sand. We set off early one Saturday morning in the summer of 1975 to cover the 250 odd miles to the Principality. Being already hardened British bike riders, we had packed a comprehensive toolkit intended to cover all eventualities.

The only thing we did not have was a tyre pump, which turned out to be a bit of an oversight. It was a warm, sunny day and everything looked rosy, until 5 miles down the winding road the bike started to give that vague wobble that meant there was a puncture in the rear wheel. We were just south of Reading at the time, in the middle of the countryside and heading for the A4 and the twisty route to Wales.

Now luckily Pete's Bonnie had the optional Quickly Detachable rear wheel, which meant we didn't have to disconnect the chain or rear brake to get the wheel out. We just had to disconnect the speedo drive, pull out the wheel spindle and out would come the wheel. So we set to it with gusto, saying things like 'good job the weather's dry and sunny' and 'lucky to get the trip's puncture out of the way so soon'. We had a puncture repair kit and tyre levers, and it

should have been a matter of ten minutes or so to find the hole in the inner tube and fix it. We carefully checked the inside of the tyre for any nails, but didn't find any. So the tyre and tube went back on the wheel, and we called in at the nearest house to borrow a pump. We were all back together and back on the road in twenty minutes – albeit with grubby hands, but we had gloves on so no one could see them. And the sun was still shining.

We burbled off down the road and eventually reached Bath. It was a nice little city and not one that we had visited before. As we wended our way out of the city centre the bike started to weave. Realizing we had our second puncture, we stopped. Sure enough the rear tyre was soft. We had passed a car spares place a few minutes earlier, so we abandoned the bike on the pavement and walked back to the shop. We bought a couple of cans of Finilec aerosol puncture repair stuff. The theory with this product is that it pumps 'goo' into the flat tyre, which then seals the hole. Magic stuff – if it works. We pumped it into the tyre, and it seemed to work. Pete shot off down the road and back to get the goo fully settled in the tyre. Just as he got back to me waiting at the side of the road, the tyre deflated. We redid the tyre with the Finilec. It went up and then deflated again as Pete came back from his second test run. We took the tools out again, removed the tube, fixed the hole (with some difficulty as the tube and the inside of the tyre were now covered in Finilec), blew up the tyre with the pressure

LEFT: *Pete Isted's 1968 T120 Bonneville pictured in 1975. The bike was pretty much standard, but Pete changed the handlebars for some Vincent straights. Note the 1968 front brake.*

RIGHT: *The rack and top box on Pete Isted's 1968 Bonneville was useful but did not enhance the handling.*

from the Finilec can, put the bike back together and set off. Two punctures in one trip – we felt a tiny bit unlucky, but the sun was still shining. We were going to hop onto the M4 motorway for about 20 miles to take the Severn Bridge over to Wales, and then follow the scenic A40 through the south of the country. So it was on to the motorway and up to 70mph.

About a mile from the bridge the bike started its now familiar weave. Pete wrestled the bike onto the hard shoulder and we started to dismantle the rear wheel with a by now finely honed level of expertise. We also started to wonder if some supernatural force was at work – maybe a puncture demon had taken up residence on the bike – because there was no possible reason for getting three punctures on one trip, was there? We set about fixing it again. The one problem with doing this on the hard shoulder was that we quickly learned not to put anything down when there was a truck thundering past: the shock of seeing the tyre levers and the spanner used to undo the speedo cable being blown up the road by the vortex caused

by a passing lorry was pretty sobering. I'd never experienced such a rush of wind, and have no desire to repeat the experience. With our increased repair skills we got the tube repaired, the tyre pumped up from the Finilec can and the wheel back on the bike pretty quickly. Three punctures in one trip – this was getting tedious, but weren't we good at repairing them! Time was pressing on. It was already midday and we hadn't even got out of England.

It was time to press on and Pete started to gun the Bonnie. Once over the bridge we picked up the A40 and motored past the 'Welcome to Wales' sign. We reached Abergavenny in the early afternoon and stopped for a late lunch. We also knew there was a bike shop there and decided that we needed to replace the inner tube at some stage as it was rather the worse for wear by now, what with the patches and the Finilec goo all over it. We bought a tube and a hand pump, and went back to the bike, sitting forlornly with its front wheel waving in the air and the rear tyre flat as a pancake. We were getting used to this by now. With a certain air of

Pete Isted's 1968 T120 in action on the road to Newgale, west Wales – a rather blurred picture taken by the author from the back of a Morris Traveller. Tony Sumner is to the right on his 175cc Montessa.

Pete Isted fitted a handlebar fairing to the Bonneville to help keep the wind off, a typical 1970s modification.

resignation we whipped out the rear wheel. Out with the old inner tube, and on with the pristine new one that would banish the puncture demon that had been sitting on the bike since Reading. We sped off. There were still about 120 miles to go, and it was now late afternoon. We had a good run and eventually drove into the campsite as twilight was falling some eleven hours after leaving home. 'This grass seems a bit slippery', Pete said as we headed for our camping pitch – then the bike started its familiar wobble and the rear tyre deflated for the fifth time that day. Luckily the campsite was next to the pub, so we left the bike in disgust and went to drown our sorrows.

It all came clear the following morning when we took the tyre off to fix the latest puncture. We examined everything closely, mainly because we had to clean off the remaining Finilec goo that covered everything. Looking at the old tube, we noticed that all four patches and the fifth puncture were on the inside – the bit that sits against the wheel rim. This was why the Finilec seemed to work, but then failed when the wheel spun: rather than being forced into a hole on the outside of the tube, it was being flung out of the hole on the inside edge. We looked to the rim – and found our puncture demon. The chrome on the inside of the rim was lifting, and sharp, raised, jagged edges were present all the way round. Talk about cause and effect – a spot of corrosion and a five-hour trip descends into farce and takes twice as long to do! There were some good points – I've only had one puncture on a bike since then (touch wood), so it seems I had my life's puncture ration in one go and I can get a TT100 off a rim so fast an F1 team should offer me a job!

After a pleasant week in the Welsh hinterlands, we set off for home, hoping there would be no more dramas. The return journey started off badly, as the Bonnie was really struggling to climb the hill out of Newgale and was generating clouds of blue smoke. Tony Sumner, behind us on his 175cc Montessa roadster, could hardly

breathe and flagged us down. Initially we feared the worst – blown rings, duff piston, dropped valve – but we discovered one of my walking boots, which was tied onto the outside of our ex-army pannier bags, had got caught up between the rear suspension unit and the tyre – the smoke had been the sole of the boot wearing away on the edge of the tyre! There was no real damage and the boots were firmly repacked. The run home was trouble-free and fast. We took the A40 out through Wales and were overtaken by one vehicle, a tatty Ford Anglia van that must have been doing over the ton when it shot past us and then went round the next bend as it was on rails. We caught up with it later when it was in convoy with a rather tasty hot-rodded Ford Popular. Its exhaust note indicated that there was a bit more than a 900cc side-valve motor in the van – it had a definite V8 burble!

Surprisingly, while the Bonnie was cruising happily at 70mph or so, Tony's Montessa kept up and ran very cool – when we stopped for fuel he had to use the choke to restart it, while the Bonnie just radiated heat like it was going out of fashion! We completed the homeward run without any problems. The Bonneville went like a train and was easily able to devour the 'A' roads at a good average speed, even though it was two-up with a load of camping gear. The seat was comfortable and there were no unscheduled stops all the way home: in fact the bike performed faultlessly. All in all, Pete's Bonnie was a great all-rounder and a trouble-free machine.

My 1970 T120R Today

The subject of the restoration documented in this book (*see* Chapter 10) is my 1970 T120R Bonneville. At the time of writing, the bike has been on the road for nine years and has covered about 1,200 miles (1,900km) per year. Having had a complete rebuild and an ongoing 'improvement programme', the bike has proved to be reliable and fun over the years. As a March 1970 model, it is one of the last of the pre oil-in-frame models. It was also built before

The author's T120R is close to standard. It just needs the proper twin horns under the tank and a new paint job. Indicators and switch gear are off a 1971–73 Triumph.

the detrimental gearbox index change of late 1970, so it really does represent the best of the 1960s breed. The bike is basically a US specification model with high handlebars and 2½ gallon fuel tank, but has had some subtle modifications, such as stainless steel mudguards, electronic ignition, indicators and alloy wheel rims to improve reliability, looks and usability.

On the road the bike comes across as eager, slightly edgy and very sharp: throttle response is excellent, the gearbox is slick and quick, and the handling and roadholding is excellent.

The first issue I had with the bike was the lack of a decent tick-over when I first took her out on the road following the restoration. I eventually traced this to one of the original carburettors. The pilot jet drillings were blocked and were pretty much impossible to clean out. By then I had read up on the carbs, and found that the Mk1 Concentric would have been just about worn out when the bike's original warranty ran out. Having replaced all of the wearing parts I didn't want to buy complete new ones, but luckily Surrey Cycles was happy to

The author's loaded Bonneville is pictured beside an old AA box in 2006.

sell me two new Concentric bodies, into which I rebuilt all my new parts.

This enabled me to tune the carburettors properly and they now give an even and reliable tick-over, as well as clean carburetion over the whole rev range. So a properly set-up pair of Concentrics can be made to work as Triumph intended. I've not bothered to fit the choke mechanisms (also known as the air sliders) as originally fitted: the carbs just need a good tickle to get the bike firing first thing, and it just doesn't need them.

Soon after getting the bike on the road I fitted the handlebar switchgear and indicators as installed from 1971. This meant adding the wiring for each indicator and sorting out which wire went where for the switches. I was also able to wire in the headlamp flasher facility, but decided against using the engine kill button on the assumption that that's just something else to go wrong. Using the 1971 switchgear also gave me some lovely alloy brake and clutch levers: one bugbear of mine is the poor quality and singularly unattractive chromed steel brake and clutch levers that Triumph fitted – alloy ones are just so much classier and feel so much nicer to use. I find the 1971 switches easy to use, but I have big hands and can see that some people could find it a bit of a stretch to the indicator toggle on the right-hand side.

I use the bike in a number of ways – quick blasts around the local area, long runs on classic meets and solo trips, and longer trips of more than 250 miles – once from home in Hampshire

RIGHT: The Bonneville makes a good tourer. Here the author's T120 takes a break on the side of the A4 at Silbury Hill, Wiltshire, in 2006.

BELOW: The wide US bars and small tank give the author's 1970 T120R the classic Triumph lean and lithe look.

to Cornwall, another from home to Pembrokeshire in Wales. The short local trips reveal the snappiness and edgy performance, while the longer trips reveal another side – the ability to cruise comfortably at 65–75mph (105–120km/h) on 'A' roads, the excellent throttle response at those cruising speeds making it a breeze to overtake dawdling traffic, and an outstanding fuel consumption of around 75mpg (3.77ltr/100km) at those cruising speeds – and on standard gear ratios as well. The only downside to the bike on tour is the seat, a new pattern item that becomes fiercely uncomfortable after 120 miles! By then it's time to fill up anyway, however, so it is not a major problem.

The bike has given very few problems after its initial restoration. Its electrics are set up with Boyer electronic ignition, a standard alternator and zener diode, and a 60 watt H4 headlamp.

The charging system copes quite happily with the headlamp and the indicators. When Rare Spares (now Tri-Cor) had a batch of new 1969–70-type front brake plates made up, I snapped up one to replace the 1968 model I had originally fitted and also bought a set of front reflectors that sit under the fuel tank. With these additions the bike is virtually standard as a Canadian market T120R. As shown here, the only visible deviations from standard specification are the lack of Windtone horns, the H4 headlamp, indicators and switchgear, and the paint job on the tank.

The only time I've had to push the bike home was when the Boyer twin coil failed about four years after fitting (I had fitted it under the tank but did not have a heat sink, so it was my fault). I replaced it with a 'standard' twin 6 volt coil setup and have had no other ignition problems.

The author's 1970 T120 contrasts with Nick Vale's 1977 T140V.

One other obscure electrical problem occurred when the bike blew its fuse a couple of times when I was using the front brake. The brake light switch is incorporated in the front brake cable, and the contacts to the switch were shorting out on the headlamp shroud. This proved a tricky one to find, but the arc marks on the inside of the shroud eventually gave it away. Rerouting and some precautionary insulation tape solved that one. The only other thing that has broken was the kick-start return spring, easily fixed with a new item, and it did provoke a change of gearbox oil.

The bike offers a pretty comfortable ride. The high US bars give an upright riding position and, as you would expect, the wind blast gets uncomfortable above 80mph, but the bike will still happily pull above 80. The bike is run on Japanese Dunlop K81 TT100 tyres and these have given excellent service in the wet and the dry, with a rear tyre lasting about 5,000 miles (8,000km) and the front giving 15,000 miles (24,000km). Brakes are excellent and I've not had any 'moments' on the bike: the front brake is powerful, fade-free and progressive, while the back one again is good, but tends to be a bit redundant when the front is in use!

The Lucas H4 headlamp, which was swiftly fitted after my first night ride with an original 40/45 watt headlamp, has been very reliable (I've not had a bulb blow for years and it lets me see where I'm going at night) and is bright enough to encourage cars to dip their lights as well. The indicators are, as far as I'm concerned, a necessity in today's traffic. The pattern Lucas items I used are cheap, but they work. I find that it pays to use some form of thread lock compound on the fixing bolts that hold the unit onto its stem, and I replace the crimped-on connector with a standard soldered-on bullet. The units are earthed through the chrome plate on the plastic body, but this has not caused any problems. I use a modern scooter two-wire flasher unit. It works very well, is cheap, reliable and robust, and is relatively insensitive to the wattage of the bulbs used, unlike the much more expensive Lucas items.

One downside of the bike is the riding position. While the seat is quite low, the footrests are quite high and can't be adjusted, so when I ride it all my weight tends to be on the seat, giving rise to a sore posterior after a hundred miles or so. This is in contrast to my BSA A65 where the footrests are adjustable, so I have a riding position in which my legs can take some of the weight, making it a lot more comfortable. The second downside is sealing the pushrod tubes. I've tried just about everything, including fitting alloy pushrod tubes, but if I leave the bike standing for a while the pushrod tubes leak. This is presumably because the seals dry out, since the tubes will seal themselves after the bike has been run for a while. Apart from the pushrod tubes,

The engine on the author's 1970 T120R is pretty much oil-tight. Alloy pushrod tubes replace the standard chromed items, and a Boyer electronic ignition replaces the points.

the bike is free of oil leaks. I suspect that the late breathing arrangement, with the engine breathing into the primary chain case, is largely responsible for the engine's oil tightness.

But these faults are minor. Apart from that, it performs well, is relatively light and manoeuvrable, is a good starter, never wet sumps and has been very reliable. It is a bike that you can use for a short burn-up or a long-distance tour with ease, and, best of all, it really looks superb!

Nick Vale's T140V

My brother Nick is the proud owner of a 1977 T140V Bonneville, a US-specification bike with the high handlebars and 2 gallon 'peanut' tank. He really likes the way it looks, since, as he says, 'even parked up I still reckon she's one of the best-looking Bonnevilles ever'. He is the fourth owner and bought the bike for a mere £500 in 1982 when it had some 10,000 miles (16,000km) on the clock. Although the bike was running when he bought it – the indicators and ignition switch were non-operational and one fork leg was seized – these were swiftly fixed with some tender loving care.

Nick has outlined his early experiences:

I was in my mid twenties when I got her and did a lot of miles in the first ten or so years. I had a Honda 400/4 as well (which had about the same performance as the Bonneville) and a Laverda Mirage for about 6 months until I wrote her off, but the Bonnie was always my favourite (and still is). She handles OK (ground clearance could be better), has lots of

Nick Vale's 1977 T140V pictured in the early 1980s, not long after he bought it. Note the non-standard exhaust.

low-down torque, and with peashooter pipes in place of the standard 'cigar' silencers she makes a lovely noise. Instrumentation is good with NVT 'Wiggly Worm' badged speedo and rev counter, the front light accepts a halogen reflector and bulb, the indicators work well and are a must for modern traffic. Left-foot gear change means no acclimatization issues when I switch to and from more modern machinery. Overall she's a good mixture of traditional character and modern convenience.

Nick used the bike hard over the years, and not only in the UK. While the fuel tank gave him a range of about 100 miles and 10 miles on reserve, it did not stop him from doing a 2,000 mile (3,200km) tour of Sweden. The only problems with the bike were a flat battery and broken speedo cable. The flat battery came about through user error, leaving the headlight on with the engine off, rather than from any underlying problem, but the speedo cable could have had a major effect on the tour:

> The broken speedo cable nearly wrecked the Swedish trip. We were pulled coming out of some little town on a clear and empty road and got written a ticket for doing 79km/h in a 40km/h limit. Not best pleased, I was relating the story to the people we were staying with, who congratulated me on my good luck. I questioned their concept of 'good luck' and they explained that Swedish speeding penalties came in three tiers: a fixed fine for up to 20km/h over, a bigger one for up to 40km/h over … and twenty-one days in clink for any higher speeds.

Owning the bike since 1982 means Nick has had lots of experience of what is needed to make it better. The rear-wheel spokes used to break regularly, a known T140V fault, and Nick solved the problem by swapping the wheel with a friend's T140E model – just before he sold it! He also fitted Boyer Bransden electronic ignition: previously he would spend an hour or so setting up the contact breakers and be rewarded

Nick Vale's T140V was a US-specification bike, but first sold in the UK. The high bars used on the T140 were a different bend to those used on the T120.

with a bike that ran superbly for about a hundred miles, but then had to reset them as the poor running returned. He has found that the Boyer kit is truly 'fit and forget' and feels it is the most important change he has made. The other significant modifications are a Norman Hyde oil cooler and an external oil filter. The Hyde cooler fits neatly between the front down-tubes, and the filter sits in front of the rear wheel. Between them they increase the oil capacity by about a pint, a significant amount given the limited oil capacity of the

ABOVE: Nick Vale's T140V now has Norton-style 'peashooter' silencers but is otherwise pretty standard.

LEFT: Nick Vale astride his T140V, 'one of the best-looking Bonnevilles ever'.

T140's frame. Norton-style peashooter silencers help to release a little extra oomph, and make a nicer sound than the standard 'cig-ar' silencers (and are a little lighter).

There have been problems over the years. The engine, for example, blew its head gasket between the bores without any obvious symp-toms, stranding Nick when he stopped for fuel and the bike wouldn't restart. He also holed a few pistons, a drive-side main bearing lost some balls, and the frame had to be welded up after it cracked at the base of the oil-tank tube. The last of these meant a full strip-down and he got the frame powder-coated at the same time, although the enamel finish on the frame was still in pret-ty good condition and much better than that on a mate's T140E, which, like my own T140E, had its powder coating peeling off in strips.

One unusual but persistent problem he had was with the oil pressure. He found there was wear on the nose of the crank that fitted into the oil seal on the timing cover, so he had it cleaned up and fitted an oversize oil seal in the timing cover. Then every few hundred miles the oil pressure would drop and inspection showed the oil seal was chewed up. Nick notes that the oil pressure light switch was the most reliable part of the lubrication system at the time! He eventually discovered that the crank was running slightly out of true, which was why the seal was getting chewed up. He realizes now that he should have checked the crank after he dropped it during the first rebuild.

Let Nick have the final words, as I could not put it better:

But I never considered selling her (I've lost count of the number of times some old codger's come up to tell me how much he'd regretted selling his Triumph for tuppence three farthing in 1960

The Cricket Green at Hartley Wintney, Hampshire, makes a good backdrop for Nick Vale's 1977 T140V and the author's 1970 T120R.

When Rockerbox rebuild an engine, they do it properly. Nick Vale's T140V unit is oil-tight, smooth and still looking good.

something). So in late 1999, with an indicated 48,000 miles on the clock, I decided to treat her to a total professional rebuild.

This I entrusted to my local Triumph garage, Rockerbox in Farnham, asking them to strip the engine and gearbox, replace anything worn beyond service limits, balance the crankshaft and do any sensible upgrades thought prudent. They went through the motor with a fine toothed comb and, unsurprisingly, announced just about everything to be worn out – so cams, bearings, seals, valves, pistons and barrels and more were all replaced and a high capacity oil pump added. About the only original bits left are the crankcases and engine mounting bolts. The job cost roughly as much as the bike is worth, and I still consider it a bargain!

She's only done a couple of thousand miles since (long gone are the 'ride her every day' days). I keep the revs (mostly) no higher than 4,000, about 70mph in top, and so far she's shown no sign of blowing up. Handling is still OK and on twisty A roads that, and the acceleration to 70, is good enough to embarrass quite a few much younger sports 600s. And even parked up I still reckon she's one of the best-looking Bonnevilles ever. My favourite.

My 1979 T140E in the 1980s

Early in 1984 I bought a 1979 T140E from a local breaker's yard in Aldershot, Hampshire. The breaker was selling it for a friend and he said that it had been used as a despatch rider's bike up in London, but needed a re-bore and top-end overhaul as it was burning a lot of oil. The bike had its head and barrel off, and the pistons and head were certainly black and coked up. Although I couldn't hear the bike running, with the engine in its half-dismantled state it was possible to check the bottom end for any play in the main bearings and the big ends, and both of them seemed fine. The bike was also missing its large plastic side-panels, and had an after-market 'two into one' exhaust, which looked quite new. But it was cheap, I could afford it and it did not look to be in too bad a condition. So the money changed hands and I had the immobile bike delivered to my home.

Initial investigation showed there was not too much wear on the pistons or the barrels, so I just fitted new piston rings (the bores were standard), cleaned up the pistons and combustion chambers, and fitted the head with new gaskets. All the electrics worked, the electronic

ABOVE: As bought in 1984 the author's 1979 T140E had its top end dismantled. All the bits were there, apart from the side panels, and with new rings the bike was a runner.

BELOW: The author's T140E came with an aftermarket '2 into 1' exhaust system. The bike ran with it on, but not very well. It did look good though!

The '2 into 1' exhaust on the author's T140E gave the drive side a bare look that, combined with the lack of side panels, emphasized the leanness of the Bonneville's lines.

ignition gave a healthy spark and the suspension was unworn – the rear shocks still damped, the swing-arm pivot was good and the front forks were fine.

With the exhaust in place the bike fired up easily and seemed to run well, passing its MoT test with no problems. Once out on the road, however, it was a different matter when using the bike in anger. With the engine topping out around 3,500rpm, all the indications were that it was running rich. Removing the air filters raised the rev limit to 4,000rpm. Although the bike was useable and looked rather smart with the 'two into one' in place, it was obvious things were not right.

The solution presented itself on a run down to my parents' place in Somerset, a fast 90-mile run down the M3 motorway and the A303. After fifty miles or so, just past Stonehenge, the exhaust spat out its baffle. I stopped, turned

round and rescued the baffle, which had by some miracle avoided being squashed by the passing traffic. With the baffle strapped onto the nifty little built-in rack ('Maximum load 15kg') the bike actually pulled up to 6,000rpm and ran a lot cleaner, with no more sooty plugs. Refitting the baffle showed that it was the exhaust system that was to blame and I began to realize that there were benefits in fitting a standard system!

Buying a new exhaust system was a problem. I wanted to use the 1971–72-style megaphone silencers, but Darrell at Rockerbox did his best to dissuade me from buying some, due to their tendency to split around the mounting brackets. I eventually bought a pattern T140E system through a contact in the trade. When fitted the bike ran perfectly, even with the air filters back in place. Cosmetically the paint on the tank was good, with a deep shine and quality pinstripes. I never bothered to replace the missing side panels as the black air filter covers looked, in my opinion, pretty good. The chrome on the wheel rims, mudguards and ancillary bits was all in good condition. The only downside was the black paint on the frame. This was the first year of the new powder-coating process and in places, especially on the front down-tubes, it was literally just falling off the frame in large strips. I pulled it off where it was loose and painted it over with black enamel where needed!

With the bike sorted, I used it daily for commuting to work (25 miles/40km each way) and for leisure at the weekend. One little quirk I found was with the Lucas Rita ignition system, which was fitted as standard. This system would generate a spark when it was first energized (that is, turned on). I tended to turn the engine off using the kill switch on the right-hand switch cluster, and then turn off the bike on the key, which was handily placed in the switch panel between the instruments. This was all well and good, unless I forgot to turn the

kill switch back to on, which happened several times when I first got the bike as I was unused to this level of sophistication. So there I would be, with the ignition switch on, kicking away while the bike stayed resolutely lifeless. After several kicks I would realize there was a problem (the bike was always a first or second kick starter) and check the kill switch, which would be off. Turning it to 'on' meant the ignition was sparked, and there would be a massive backfire as the fuel in the exhaust ignited. This happened once when I was visiting my cousin. When I tried to leave shortly before midnight, there was a terrific backfire and I must have woken up half of Slough! My cousin was certainly impressed by the noise, but had to fend off questions from his neighbours the following morning.

One trip with the bike really stands out. Peter Isted, whose 1968 T120 Bonneville is featured above, had graduated to owning a Ducati 900SS. One Saturday morning he dropped around to

Once the '2 into 1' exhaust had been replaced with a standard '2 into 2' system the T140E ran brilliantly. The bike was smooth, reliable and comfortable.

ask if I wanted to go to the Ducati Owners' Club Tenth Anniversary Rally, which was being held in a field somewhere near Bath. With nothing else to do, I said yes, and we set off on a leisurely ride down the A4 to the rally site, Pete on his Duke and I on the T140E. It was about 90 miles (145km) in total. When we arrived we found that the site was next door to a great-looking pub and the rally was a two-day event. So we decided to camp overnight. There was one slight problem: we hadn't bought any camping gear with us. So it was a quick flit back to base to pick up tent, sleeping bag and spare underpants. And when I say quick, I mean quick. The Ducati 900SS is a fast bike, and so is the Bonneville on the right roads. The A4 could have been built for both bikes – lots of fast single track with wide lanes, good surfaces, gentle bends and light traffic meant Pete and I could really press on. I swear that my speedo hardly read below 90mph all the way home. The bike performed faultlessly, keeping pace

with Pete and only losing out slightly on the long fast stretches of road. Around the corners, the Bonnie's breaking and acceleration gave no problems with keeping up with Pete, and the bike felt fine at the end of 90 very quick miles – still ticking over and showing no signs of distress. It didn't miss a beat and didn't leak a drop of oil there or back! The rally was a success, very enjoyable (bikes, camping and a good pub – the perfect combination) and I didn't get lynched by the Ducati Mafia (just) despite trying to persuade them that the Triumph was a zero (or was it 360) degree V-twin.

All good things have to come to an end, though, and with winter approaching, and with a 50-mile (80km) round trip to work, I wimped out and swapped the Triumph for an MGB sports car. But my abiding memories of the bike are of a reliable, smooth and fast machine with fine handling, good quality ancillaries and a strong engine that was able to keep up with one of the finest pedigree sports bikes then available.

The author's T140E from the timing side. The new standard exhaust looks good, and the missing side panels give the bike the look of an earlier T140V.

Darrell Babkirk's 1987 Harris Bonneville

Darrell Babkirk of Rockerbox owns a 1987 'Harris' Bonneville, one of the last made. He is the second owner and bought it in 2003, with about 2,000 miles on the clock. Over the past four years he has put another couple of thousand on the clock, but he is keeping the bike 'for best', doing most of his mileage on his Harley. As a lifelong Triumph fan, Darrell relishes owning one of the last of the line and finds the bike superb. It runs smoothly with punchy acceleration, and he reckons that the motor is one of the best Bonneville units he has come across.

The handling and roadholding are excellent and the electrics (standard three-phase alternator and Lucas Rita ignition) have never faltered. The Avon Roadrunners were fitted as standard and are the originals. He is especially impressed with the rear brake mechanism and the air filter boxes and side-panel assemblies. The rear brake master cylinder is mounted high up on the rear frame tube, out of the way of the dirt and grime that ruin the Meriden units, while the air filter boxes fit correctly and do not leak, making it a lot easier to set up the Amal Mk1½ carbs. Stainless steel mudguards front and rear are rot-free and low maintenance. The only downsides are the front forks and the wheel rims. The Paioli front forks work well, but it is difficult to get spares for them – Darrell's currently have some weeping from the seals. Darrell has had them rebuilt once and they were found to be insanely complex internally. The Radaelli wheel rims also came from Italy, and the chrome on them is poor. Oh, and while they work well, the handlebar switches are the same Magura items fitted to Indian Enfields!

Darrell Babkirk and his Harris Bonneville outside Rockerbox. The bike has an earlier US-specificatiom 2 gallon fuel tank custom painted in black and silver.

The bike also exhibits some interesting changes from what is supposed to be the 'standard' specification fitted by the factory. The bike has German-made alloy 'Nikasil' barrels, which were originally painted black. The clue to the fitment of these barrels is the use of studs and nuts as the outer head fixings rather than the bolts used on the standard cast-iron barrels – you don't want to be screwing steel bolts in and out of the alloy barrels if possible. A second feature is the use of 1971–72-style rocker boxes with the small round tappet adjuster covers. Darrell has confirmed with Harris that the factory ran out of the T140-style units with the larger bolt-on covers and had to fit the earlier type towards the end of production. This feature really confuses the rivet counters at shows when they try to work out exactly what the bike's origins are.

When he bought the bike it came with a 'Meriden'-badged Veglia rev counter, a rare feature fitted only to very late Meriden bikes, but the speedometer was not badged – so he had to get a matching speedometer built up to keep the symmetry! He also wonders if the bike

ABOVE: Darrell's Harris Bonneville came with early 650cc-type rocker boxes with the round tappet covers. These were on the bike from new, and illustrate how risky it is to rely on the documented specifications.

BELOW: The Harris Bonnevilles had the T140E-style instrument panel. Darrell's instruments sport the rare 'Meriden' logo used on late Co-op produced bikes.

The Harris Bonneville sports Norton 'peashooter' silencers – a popular modification today. They look and sound good, and are lighter than the standard units.

has the TSS-style crank, but has not investigated that far.

Darrell does not want to keep the bike standard. While he appreciates it for what it is, he is not blind to its faults and has a programme of improvements in hand to make the bike into his ultimate Bonnie. The most obvious change is the exhaust system. He has replaced the huge and quiet Italian Lafranconi silencers with Norton 'peashooter'-styled units and has also replaced the original balance pipe-equipped exhaust pipes with new individual pipes. The new silencers enable the engine to breathe more easily, and with the decent air boxes and set-up by Arthur (also of Rocker-box) the engine runs and ticks over faultlessly. The original Paioli rear shocks have been replaced with Meriden-type Girling units and the rear grab rail is a 1980 T140E unit with its small but useful built-in carrier.

Handlebars are the classic bend from a US-specification 1967 TR6C. Finally the tank is a Meriden T140 1976 or 1977 US export peanut model, sporting 1970s 'Eyebrow' tank badges and Darrell's own specification silver over black paint job, while the seat is a 'King and Queen' custom aftermarket unit made by Fox, with the traditional Triumph logo embossed in the cover.

Darrell, however, has not yet finished with the Bonnie. He has a vision of what he wants the bike to be like and is steadily taking it on the journey to achieving it. Starting at the front, he is proposing to replace the troublesome Paioli forks with a T140 unit and will fit a single front disc, but with an alloy Lockheed racing calliper, which should match the current braking power of the twin Brembo discs fitted as standard. The T160-style instrument console will go, to be replaced with a custom CNC machined alloy bracket used to carry the speedometer and tachometer in rubber caps, as were fitted from 1971 to 1977. He will, however, retain the original and rare 'Meriden'-badged units. To complete the classic look for the front end, a traditional chrome headlamp carrying the warning lights will be mounted on chrome T140 rubber-mounted headlamp 'ears'. The front mudguard will also be changed for a slimmer, more attractive one, although the Harris stainless guard would fit the Lockheed forks. The wheel rims with their dodgy chrome will be changed for a set of Akront alloy rims he already

has 'in stock', and he will tidy up the rear end by replacing the T140E grab rail with an earlier version and fit a 1967 US-specification alloy rear light.

All in all, Darrell really likes his Bonnie, but he recognizes it can be improved. With careful picking from the Triumph parts bins, he is building it to his interpretation of the ultimate Bonnie. Currently it is a fine machine, and with the proposed improvements it will become his interpretation of what the Bonnie should have been.

The twin-disc front end on the Harris Bonneville looks good and works well, but spares for the forks are getting hard to find.

10 Restoration

Firstly, a word about safety. The following chapter describes the methods and techniques that I use to restore a bike. Anyone who embarks on such a project should be aware that there are dangers associated with working on old bikes. This warning is important as old oil, petrol and other fluids used in old bikes can be toxic, there

is a strong likelihood that the brakes will have asbestos in the shoes and in the dust in the drums, and there is a constant risk of injury from sharp tools and bits of bike. Anyone who decides to restore their own bike should only do jobs that they are competent to do, and take all safety precautions that are needed. If in doubt, ask an expert.

As I have said a number of times before in my other books – the first part of any restoration is find a bike. I had decided that I wanted to restore a pre oil-in-frame 650cc Triumph twin and would try to find one from the final years of production between 1968 to 1970. I suspected that I would end up with an ex-police Saint, as my budget was pretty tight. I scanned the classified adverts in the classic bike press for a couple of months, but there were precious few projects, and even fewer Triumph projects. It seemed that most of the bikes advertised were 'good runners' and 'fully restored' – those that weren't were 'very original' and 'unrestored' – and all of them were demanding prices much higher than I was intending to spend. So I switched to 'Plan B' – start talking to the classic bike dealers.

This approach soon turned up some results. The best project I could find was a 1970 T120R, re-imported from the USA as part of a container-load of bikes. Most of them were complete, but this one was in a bit of a state. The engine was fixed loosely in the frame, the fuel tank, oil tank and side panel were dented and it had a rough red paint job put on with the traditional yard broom. The front wheel had an early non-flanged straight spoke hub and the front

When bought, the author's 1970 T120R Bonneville was in need of some tender loving care. But the frame and engine numbers matched, and most of the bike was present.

The wiring is virtually non-existent, and there are no coils, battery or even a headlamp!

While the wiring is a real mess, the engine is complete. Both carburettors are present, as is the tachometer drive.

forks were in pieces. Most of the big bits were there, however, and so were most of the smaller fittings, including the carburettors, a Smiths magnetic speedometer (albeit a 1975/76 NVT 'Wiggly Worm' logo instrument in a pretty poor state), all the underseat battery tray gubbins, the front footrests and rear brake pedal. The electrics were a truly awesome mess, with no coils, bits of a rectifier, no horns and a comprehensibly wrecked wiring loom. The front forks were in bits and the stanchions were rusty and pitted, but the legs and yokes (triple trees) were present and, as it turned out, correct. The rear wheel was there and in one piece, but the front wheel was an early type with a non-flanged hub. Mudguards were incorrect Japanese chromed items, and the front mudguard stays and rear grab rail were missing. Surprisingly the engine and frame

numbers matched, and the engine did not look as if it had been messed with: all the external fasteners were in good condition, with no rounded heads or chisel marks on the casings. There were a couple of fins missing from the barrel but the cylinder head fins were all present and correct. Despite this apparently depressing picture, I felt that the bike had potential and the price was right. The money changed hands and the bike was mine. With the front forks and wheels not attached, it fitted easily in my brother's estate car and I soon had it home.

What Have I Got?

The first part of my restoration methodology is to work out roughly what is needed, mainly to identify anything that is difficult to get hold of, and then to concentrate on getting a rolling chassis up together. This means that most of the bits I buy can be hung on the frame, avoiding the classic restoration issues of losing things you've already bought, or damaging new bits when storing them in the garage. On this occasion the main missing items that would influence the strategy were the mudguards, and I would also need to find a replacement front hub. At this stage I sent off for a genuine Triumph workshop manual and a parts book from JR Publications, and I started to buy books on the Bonneville. Probably the best one was David Gaylin's *Triumph Motorcycle Restoration Guide: Bonneville and TR6, 1956–1983*, an incredibly comprehensive survey of the T120 and TR6 US models, closely followed by J. R. Nelson's *Bonnie*, which charts the development history of the Bonneville.

The second consideration was to decide what I would use the bike for once complete, since this would dictate the standard of the restoration. I decided that I would use the bike to ride, and so would put practicality above originality, and not strive for a *concours* finish, Rather, I would aim for the sort of finish that it would have as it originally came from the factory. The practicality aspect meant that I would use stainless fittings where possible and modern electronics where needed, so producing a bike that I hoped could be driven throughout the year without needing too much work to keep going, and would not be too affected by the salty roads of a UK winter.

Frame and Suspension

The frame and all its fittings were stripped, with pictures taken to record where all the various brackets and parts went, and the parts book consulted to identify any missing bits. There were surprisingly few, reinforcing my opinion that the bike, despite its appearance, was a good basis for restoration. Very few parts that came off the frame showed much corrosion or abuse,

In fact the engine appears to be in good condition. Although the fasteners are rusty, they do not have many witness marks on them, implying the motor may not have been taken apart.

and any rust evident was usually just minor surface rust. The frame, once stripped of its components, was split into the main loop and rear sub-frame, and it and the swinging arm, oil tank and side panel were consigned to the shot blasters for cleaning and powder coating in black.

With these bits out of the way, I could rebuild the forks so that when the frame came back I could quickly get a rolling chassis built up. The forks were pretty straightforward, if not cheap. I had the yokes and the legs, but just about everything else needed replacing. Luckily all parts were available off the shelf from my various suppliers. These included stanchions, bushes, shuttle valves, springs, gaiters, seals and fork-seal holders. Stainless steel cap nuts, fork stem sleeve nut and top and bottom yoke pinch bolts replaced the damaged and corroded originals and promised to give good service and not to rust. I stripped the paint off the legs, and resprayed them using black Smoothite, an excellent paint that gives a lovely tough and original-looking finish. With the fork legs reassembled and the yokes resprayed black, the forks were ready to go in when the frame came back from being powder-coated. The finishing touches to the front forks were a new chrome headlamp shell, with the correct holes for the ammeter and two warning lights (oil pressure and main beam), two new top covers to carry the headlamp, and a new instrument mounting bracket to carry the soon to be acquired speedometer and tachometer.

With the frame back from the powder-coaters, and new taper roller head races driven into the frame's headstock, the forks fitted and the rear sub-frame bolted on, the chassis was back together but not yet rolling. To continue work I fixed the frame onto a wooden box on the garage floor by screwing a piece of wood across the lower frame rails, holding it in place while the forks, swinging arm and other minor refurbished components were bolted onto it.

The frame looks straight and all the under-seat components are present. The battery carrier and oil tank rubber mounts are badly perished.

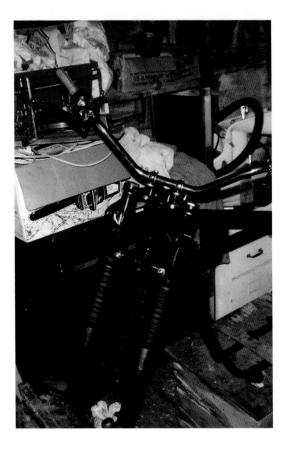

Up on the bench, the first thing to be fitted to the newly blasted and powder-coated frame is the rebuilt forks. Only the yokes and sliders are reusable: new stanchions, springs, gaiters, seal holders, top nuts and headlamp shrouds are needed.

Wheels

For the original restoration, I initially rebuilt the wheels with new galvanized spokes, but kept the original steel rims (19in front and 18in rear). While the front rim was in pretty good shape, the chrome on the rear rim was not good. It looked as if it had worn off rather than flaked off, but despite this the rim was not rusty as the plating under the chrome was still present. Building wheels is a task that is often farmed out by the restorer, but I find it a satisfying activity in its own right, as long as you have the right spokes and rim to build onto the hub.

In the Bonneville's case the wheels were complete, but the front hub was wrong – it was an early Triumph front hub without the extended spoke flange on the brake side allowing for the full width of the hub to be used for braking. Once a correct hub was bought second-hand from Rockerbox, the rebuild of the front wheel with new spokes was carried out. The rear wheel was not the Triumph quick-detachable type, so the rear brake drum had to be detached from the hub before the spokes on the drive side could be replaced. The hub is held on to the drum with six bolts and associated nuts and washers. Once the hub is detached from the drum, the spokes are easily slotted into position and the wheel can be built. I felt that the rear rim let down the bike's appearance, however, and a couple of years after the restoration I replaced the steel rims with flanged alloy ones, using stainless steel spokes to make up a set of relatively low maintenance and durable wheels. It is these spokes and rims that I've used to illustrate the wheel rebuild.

The technique I used was to loosely build each wheel, getting all the spokes in place and then truing up the wheels, before finally tightening the spokes to an acceptable level.

The front hub had two different types of spoke: one straight pull for the left-hand side, and one with a 90-degree bend on the hub end to fit the brake-side flange. Each side has twenty

The first row of spokes in place on the front wheel. The flanged alloy rims were added by the author a couple of years after the original restoration.

The second row of spokes in place on the front hub. The flange side has to be done first as the straight pull spokes on the other side of the hub interfere with the flange-side spokes, and make it difficult to get them into position.

spokes, ten of which face 'forwards' and ten 'back'. Note that, on the Triumph flanged front hub, the inner spokes must be in tension when the brake is applied. For the front hub I started by putting the 'back'-facing spokes into the flanged side, and loosely connected them into the correctly dimpled hole in the rim. Each spoke was positioned in each fourth hole in the rim.

Next I put all the 'forward'-facing spokes in the flange side of the hub, and again loosely fitted them to the other correct hole in the rim, in this case the middle hole of the three holes between the first set of spokes. This left every other hole in the rim free to take the spokes from the other (non-flanged) side of the hub. The reason I did the flanged side first was that the spokes on the other side of the hub were 'straight pull' and hence could be fed directly into the hub, so the spokes on the flange side did not interfere with them on assembly.

With all of the flange-side spokes in place, the wheel could be turned over and the other side's spokes could be fixed in place.

As the non-flanged side spokes were 'straight pull', they were easily inserted into the holes in the hub and headed straight for the correct hole in the rim, which made life easy and quick. With all of the spokes loosely connected, the wheel was starting to look complete. It now needed to be trued up. To do this I used an old BSA C15 swinging arm, which I held upright in the Black & Decker Workmate, placing the wheel in the fork ends.

To get all the spokes to a similar level of tightness, and thus pull the wheel into an initial shape, I used a handheld drill with a variable torque setting to screw each spoke nipple onto the spoke. Set at the lowest torque setting, this quickly had the desired result. I then checked the wheel for 'roundness' by spinning the wheel and marking where it went up and down. Spokes on the 'low' side were loosened, and those on the 'high' side tightened, which moved the rim in relation to the hub. This operation was continued until the wheel was running true. I could then set the correct offset. In the Triumph's case the front-wheel rim needs to be

Nearly there – both sides of spokes are in and the wheel now needs to be trued up.

RIGHT: *The rebuilt forks are a ready-made jig to check the wheel alignment and to make any adjustments needed to get the wheel running true.*

BELOW: *And this is what you need to check for once the wheel build is complete. Any excess spoke poking through the nipple must be ground down level, otherwise a puncture is inevitable.*

central to the centre of the hub, and any side-to-side play was sorted by spinning the wheel and marking where the rim was out of true. By loosening spokes on the 'near' side and tightening the spokes on the 'far' side, the rim could be pulled straight so that it ran true.

With the rim running true, the spokes can then all be tightened: if you give every spoke the same amount of tightening using a spoke key or spanner on the nipple, then the wheel should stay true. If, having tightened the spokes up to a suitable level, the rim is taken out of true, you will need to repeat the above steps to re-true the wheel. Final truing can also be carried out with the wheel mounted in the frame or the front forks. This is also a useful test to make sure that the offset of the wheel is correct (the wheel is running centrally in the bike and is not offset).

The final operation on the wheel is to check if there are any spokes protruding through the nipples. Any that are must be cut down to the level of the spoke nipple, as any protrusions will cause punctures, with potentially disastrous consequences. It is vital to do this, and I grind them down using a Dremmel-type mini tool.

With the wheels completed, I was able to fit new Japanese Dunlop K81 TT100 tyres. While originally the Bonneville was equipped with Dunlop K70 or Avon Speedmaster tyres, the

With the wheels built, the rolling chassis can be assembled. Once the mudguards are on the project is starting to look like a bike.

TT100s were the top-of-the-range tyre in 1970, and I decided that only the best was good enough for my bike! With the tyres on, brakes had to be sorted. The rear brake was the standard 7in (178mm) single leading shoe item, and just needed new brake shoes, brake shoe springs and a new return spring on the operating lever. The brake drum was cleaned up, painted black and bolted onto the hub with eight new bolts. The brake backplate was cleaned up and painted, and the whole mechanism reassembled. As the bike was to a US specification, the rear sprocket was bolted onto the drum, rather than being cast as part of the drum, so a new one was fixed on. I also bought a stainless steel brake rod and new adjuster bullet. The front brake was a bit more of a problem, as I wanted a twin leading shoe backplate. I eventually tracked one down at a reasonable price. This was a 1968 unit, but came

with the 1969/70 bell-crank operating arms. I eventually found some new old-stock operating arms, but the only ones available were BSA items, which of course are identical in everything bar the part number. So a good tip when restoring a BSA or a Triumph: check if the part you need has two part numbers and quote both. Most dealers will be able to sort them out but it is less hassle for them if you supply both numbers. So with the brake refurbished, again with new shoes and springs, the brake plate could be united with the hub. Another tip – make sure you tighten up the central nut that holds the brake plate onto the hub, since it is inaccessible once the wheel is in the forks. With the brakes done, the wheels were complete and the rolling chassis could be built up. This meant that the bike was starting to look like a motorcycle and it became easy to roll around the garage.

Tinware

The oil tank, battery carrier and side panel were the next things to be fitted. The oil tank and side panel had been blasted and powder-coated. Some people say this is a bad move, but as long as you clean out all of the grit from the oil tank there should be no problem; I use solvent, followed by lots of water and detergent, and keep at it until there is nothing but air in the tank. Powder coating gives a good tough finish to the tank and panel, which will stand the test of time. The two battery tray carriers and the battery tray itself were painted with Smoothite and refitted with new rubber 'top hat' mouldings on the drive side (a good tip is to use some rubber lubricant to fit these as it makes the job really easy) and bolted onto the timing-side lugs. The battery carrier then just slots over the two crosspieces (or front and rear straps, according to the parts book) and is fixed in position with a sleeved nut that also acts as an anchor for the battery strap. A new rubber mat on the base completed the battery carrier. The top of the oil tank is mounted on two frame lugs using top-hat rubbers and studs, and the base is fixed using a rubber grommet that sits on a peg on a 'C'-shaped bracket that bolts to the frame. On the 1970 bikes the side panel has two inserts in its rear edge that take rubber top-hat grommets that simply locate on two pegs on the rear frame. It is secured in place by a screw with a large black plastic knurled ring in the top of the front edge, which enables it to be undone without tools. The toolkit sits in a platform inside the panel.

The next job was to fit the mudguards or, as our American cousins call them, fenders. I had decided to use stainless guards for a number of reasons. I do not like painted mudguards as the paint is prone to damage around fixings, especially on a parallel twin with its vibration. On a purely personal level, I also think chromed or stainless steel looks much better than any paint job. Stainless steel guards were also standard fitment to Canadian T120 models in 1970 (and for the US T120 in 1968, and the TR6C from 1967 to 1970), so it was not going too non-standard. At the time of the restoration stainless guards of the correct shape and form were readily available and, while more expensive than mild steel, did not need painting. One slight problem that I had was that the guards I bought were undrilled, and it was the most nerve-racking part of the restoration to drill the guards to ensure they fitted correctly. With the wheels complete, it gave me a reference to centre the guards and ensure they followed the lines of the wheels as well. Fitting the rear guard was carried out starting from the front bracket, which was bolted into two lugs on the swinging arm lug. This bracket has a single hole in it to bolt it to the guard. This fixing defined the position of all the other fixings. Using masking tape on the guard, I used a pencil to mark the location of the first hole after fitting the guard to the bike and manoeuvring it around until it was square and positioned correctly. Then I removed the guard, drilled the hole and fixed it back in place. Centre punching and drilling the holes with the masking tape in place meant that there was less chance of damaging the finish on the guards, and using a drill slightly larger than ¼in (6.4 mm) gave a bit of 'wriggle room' to allow for errors. With the first fixing in place I moved to the next in line, which was the bridge piece between the top shock-absorber mounts. Again, marking up the position on the masking tape made it easy to punch and drill the holes. Replacing the guard with its two fittings bolted up, I repeated the process for the clip that fits over the rear frame rail, and finally drilled the holes for the fixing to the rear lifting handle. At each stage it is vital to check alignment and positioning. The process was repeated for the front guard, using black-painted stays: Triumph specified chromed stays for painted guards and black stays for stainless guards. I fitted the front stay first, being careful to make sure the guard was centralized between the fork legs and to the wheel, as any errors will stand out, and that the two holes for the stay were equal distances from the centre and square to the edge of the guard. Next I fitted the top stay, again making sure the holes were correctly positioned and that the stay was parallel to the fork legs. Finally the rear stay was fitted by bolting it up to the fork legs and offering it up to the rear of the mudguard and marking out the position of the final two holes. The end result was a set of perfectly fitting guards. I used stainless steel ¼ UNF bolts, stainless washers and self-locking nuts to fix the guards permanently in place, giving a maintenance- and rust-free assembly. The final bit of drilling was needed to fit the rear light assembly and number plate brackets onto the rear mudguard, which was achieved with the guard in place.

Engine, Primary Drive and Gearbox

With the rolling chassis completed, I turned to the motor. When I collected the bike the engine was in the frame and was apparently all there, but as there was no chain or kick-starter it was impossible to assess its condition. So, I set to disassembling the engine on the bench. The first thing I found was that the head bolts were all loose, which raised my suspicions about the state of the internals. With the head off, inspection of the valve gear showed it was all in good condition, and the valve seats showed no signs of wear or recession. One of the screw-in exhaust ports was loose, so the head had to go off to Rockerbox to be re-threaded.

With the barrels off, the pistons look awful – but they are standard and will clean up well. The bore is well within tolerances, so new rings are all that are needed.

Once the engine is on the bench and the barrels off, the damaged small end can clearly be seen. Fortunately the rest of the engine is in good condition.

With the primary chain case off the engine turned over easily, so at least it was not seized, but close inspection showed that one piston had some up and down play. Removing the barrels showed a shot small-end. Most of the remains of the bronze bearing was recovered from the sump filter. The good news was that the barrels were on standard bore, and the pistons were in good condition, although fairly heavily carboned up, so the barrel got its glaze busted with some emery paper and new rings went onto the list of bits to get.

The shot small-end had enlarged the conrod eye, consigning it to the scrap bin. This was bad news, as I would have to strip down the motor in its entirety to ensure that all the bits of bush were cleaned out. On reflection, however, I would strip down any engine that I had no history for, just to be on the safe side, and on a bike with a sludge trap in the crank this is a must. The engine showed no sign of being previously stripped. All the fasteners were in good condition and there were no signs of bodging or butchery on the cases. The gearbox and primary drive were both removed and inspected and no problems were found with either of them, although I replaced the clutch friction plates and springs as the originals were worn. With the cases split I could remove the crank

and check the big-ends. These seemed to be unworn and were still on the original shell sizes. Overall the engine had very little wear and I surmised that the bike had been run until the small-end went, possibly quite early in the bike's life, and had then been slung into a shed or barn. The crank and crankcases I packed off to Rockerbox so that Arthur the mechanic could check the crank, clean the sludge trap and install new main bearings. Arthur emphasized that you should not use an impact driver on the old sludge-trap screw, as this can stress the crank and result in breakage across the drive-side big-end journal. When Arthur removed the sludge trap it was blocked solid. It had evidently been doing its job, but the big-ends would probably have been starved of oil pretty soon if the small-end had not gone first – so that was good timing by the engine. Arthur replaced the slotted-head sludge-trap plug with a socket-headed version, which would be much easier to remove in the future. Rockerbox also supplied a set of second-hand conrods, and new big-end bolts and nuts to fit. I polished the conrods to eliminate any possibility of stress cracks and also made sure that both piston and conrod sets were, as far as possible, equal in weight. Putting the engine back together was straightforward, but I made sure that it was done in the

The drive side are in good condition. New clutch plates and springs are all that are needed. Even the original primary chain is in good condition and may be reused.

cleanest possible environment. I cleaned and then oiled everything before reassembly, and used colloidal graphite paste on all moving parts, such as cylinder walls, piston rings, big-end bearings and valve stems. This gives the parts a working skin that is self-lubricating and will retain oil, giving the new parts extra protection during the initial stages of running in.

With the cases back together and the barrels on, I inspected the gearbox internals for wear or pitting, and the cam plate and selector forks for any wear. They were all fine, so I was able to reassemble the gearbox with the original parts. The only tricky part was to index the box correctly but, following the procedure outlined in the manual, it took only two tries to have a box with all four gears in place.

The primary drive assembly was straightforward. I fitted a second-hand encapsulated alternator stator and rotor, and new clutch plates and springs. I could then replace the assembled engine in the frame. I left the assembly of the top-end until after the engine was in the frame, since the extra clearance without the head in place meant it was a lot easier to get the engine in the frame, even with the 1970 front engine

plates. When fitting the engine bolts, don't tighten any of them up until they are all in place. You should fit the underside stud first, followed by the rear plates and finally the front plates (on the 1970 Bonnie; earlier ones have a lug and single bolt fixing). Inserting the lower engine stud is easy if a tapered drift of the correct diameter is used. Drive in the drift to locate the engine and then use the stud to drive out the drift, inserting the spacers between the frame and engine as it goes. This avoids damaging the stud's threads, as can occur if you just drive it in. Fixing the rear engine plates is fiddly. Make sure the footrest hangers are firmly bolted in place on the plates before you fit them. Some Locktite or similar on the footrest bolts is a good idea as they are almost impossible to get at once the engine plates are on. Finally, on the 1970 bikes the front engine plates can be bolted up using the two bolts through the frame and the stud and two nuts for the engine front lug. Then you can go round and tighten up all the bolts. Loose engine bolts not only mean vibration, but they may fret and damage the soft alloy cases and the holes in the frame, so make sure they are all tight.

With the engine firmly bolted into place, the head is easy to bolt on. One point to note when fitting the head is that it is really important to check the clearances needed for the pushrod tube gaskets. The silicon rubber rings are available in various thicknesses and it is important to check that the ones you fit have the required 'extra' thickness to crush properly on assembly. With the pushrod tubes and seals in place the cylinder head can be bolted loosely in place. With the pushrods located on the tappets, the engine should be rotated until inlet or exhaust pushrods are both down, and then the relevant rocker box can be bolted into position avoiding putting any strain on the smaller fittings. When both boxes are in place the head can be

New carburettor bodies are fitted when the orginals prove to be too gummed up. No choke mechanism is fitted, nor is it needed.

torqued down and then the small screws around each rocker box periphery can be given a final tighten. With the head steady, bolted to the rocker-box studs, and the engine mounts tightened up, the engine is in place.

Two Amal Concentric 930 carburettors that came with the bike were the correct type, so I stripped them down and cleaned them, replaced the slides, jets, floats, float valves and needles, and carefully reassembled them. They were bolted onto the flanges on the head using rubber washers under the nuts. A new fuel hose and clips were used, along with new taps for the fuel tank. I used chrome-plated slides, since these tend not to wear out the carburettor bodies, unlike the original zinc alloy ones.

With the engine in and fully assembled, the next job was to fit the breather-pipe fittings. The 1970 Bonneville engine had discarded the timed breather valve on the end of the inlet camshaft and breathed directly into the primary chain case. The chain case is vented by a large tube running from a plastic adaptor on the top rear of the case. This tube fits into a 'T' piece to connect the breather pipe to the oil tank vent. The main 'D'-section breather tube runs from the 'T' piece back along the edge of the rear mudguard, and terminates at the end of the guard behind the number plate. It is silver coloured, with a 'U'-shaped section, and is fixed to the outside edge of the rear mudguard using four 'P' clips, which required more nerve-racking drilling to fix them to the mudguard.

The final part of the jigsaw was to do the wiring. As the bike was going to be pretty much standard, I bought a new wiring loom and draped it over the bike as a starting point. The loom followed the standard wiring colours and fitted very well, and by being methodical and addressing each circuit in turn – front light, rear light, charging, and ignition – it was a relatively easy task.

Once a circuit was connected up, I would check to see that everything was working before going on to the next. A couple of items were

ABOVE: *The electrics are standard, with a new zener diode mounted in the heat sink under the headlamp where it gets plenty of cooling air. All the transfers for the Bonneville are still available: note the 'World Motorbike Speed Record Holder' transfer under the ignition switch.*

non-standard. I was using a solid state rectifier (cheaper and more reliable than the selenium plate type originally fitted, and also more efficient with lower current losses), so needed to run an additional earth from the unit to the battery. This was no great problem as the unit was bolted onto the back of the battery tray, and the Boyer ignition used a single, two-ended coil that needed only slight modifications to the original wiring diagram. I omitted the horn relay, as I did not have the original Lucas Windtone horns, and just fitted an aftermarket Japanese unit, which was loud, small, did not need a relay and still works. With an ammeter in the headlamp, along with the two warning lights (oil pressure and main beam) and the three-position toggle light switch, the inside of the headlamp was a bit crowded. It was even more so when I fitted the flasher unit in there as well, but it all fitted with a bit of persuasion. In return for a few pints of beer my brother-in-law had painted the tank to give a deep orangey red, two-pack finish with a deep shine to it – not standard but very cheap! A new-pattern seat replaced the original that came with the bike and was in a pretty poor state. Finally I fitted the fuel tank with all new bolts and studs.

The Bonneville completed – and looking good. The bike is MoT tested and ready for the road. I've not yet fitted indicators and later Triumph handlebar switches.

Running and Testing

With the bike completed, it was time to get it fired up and on the road. With a new battery the bike fired up on about the third kick and seemed to be running alright, but with a bit of a hit or miss tick-over. With all new (and very stiff) leathers, helmet, boots and gloves I rode off to the MoT test. The unreliable tick-over made it a bit of a baptism of fire but the bike passed. I then had to get it registered before I could ride it on the road, a task I left to the dealer from

Another shot of the completed bike. Note the 1968 front brake plate: I later replaced it with the correct 1969/70 bell-crank version.

whom I bought the original wreck. In a few weeks the documentation arrived and I was on the road.

The whole restoration went very smoothly. It was greatly facilitated by the almost 100 per cent availability of spares and loads of background information available for the big Triumphs. The bike itself was actually in pretty good condition and no major remedial work was needed to repair any bodges. Maybe I was lucky, but my experience shows that the big Triumph twins make a great restoration project.

LEFT: The underseat layout on the completed restoration. This makes a bit of a contrast to how it was when I bought the bike! Note the transfers and the square solid-state rectifier.

BELOW: The bike's handlebar layout as it is today. The high and wide US-specification handlebars carry 1971–73 switchgear to operate the indicators. A small quartz clock nestles between the black-faced Smiths speedometer and tachometer.

APPENDIX
The Numbers

This section attempts to unravel the Triumph numbering system and identify which numbers were assigned. The information is based on a number of sources, including J. R. Nelson's *Bonnie*, Harry Woolridge's *The Triumph Trophy Bible* and *Triumph Speed Twin & Thunderbird Bible*, David Gaylin's *Triumph Motorcycle Restoration Guide* and the various brochures and technical publications issued by Triumph during the period.

Engine and Frame Numbers

Triumph's first numbering system was simple: numbers were prefixed with 'DU' and ran from 101 upwards. There was just one run of numbers, with the type of bike being identified by a model prefix, such as 6T for the Thunderbird. The accompanying tables identify how the numbers were allocated to the 650cc 6T, TR6 and T120 up to 1973, when the 650cc machines were superseded by the 750cc models.

Triumph 6T Thunderbird Engine and Frame Numbers				
Model year	*6T start no.*	*6T finish no.*	*6T start date*	*6T finish date*
1963	DU764	DU5824	19/12/62	15/08/63
1964	DU6329	DU13210	16/10/63	04/08/64
1965	DU14635	DU24874	7/09/64	6/08/65
1966	DU25877	DU44393	23/08/65	28/08/66

Triumph TR6 Trophy and Tiger Engine and Frame Numbers				
Model year	*TR6 start no.*	*TR6 finish no.*	*TR6 start date*	*TR6 finish date*
1963	DU102	DU5790	29/09/62	14/08/63
1964	DU6127	DU13287	29/08/63	05/08/64
1965	DU14226	DU23732	27/08/64	21/06/65
1966	DU24876	DU43161	6/08/65	8/07/66
1967	DU46201	DU66246	14/09/66	3/07/67
1968	DU68364	DU85903	9/08/67	26/06/68
1969	DU87124	DU88524	29/07/68	14/08/68
− *then* (1969)	NC02352	not known	26/10/68	15/07/69
1970	HD23795	ND60540	9/07/69	8/10/70

continued overleaf

Triumph TR6 Trophy and Tiger Engine and Frame Numbers (*continued*}

Model year	TR6 start no.	TR6 finish no.	TR6 start date	TR6 finish date
1971	PE03157	HE29817	3/11/70	8/07/71
1972	JG33084	EG57252	20/08/71	17/05/72
1973 (650)	JH15475	JH15596	18/08/72	Sept 72

Triumph T120 Bonneville Engine and Frame Numbers

Model year	T120 start no.	T120 finish no.	T120 start date	T120 finish date
1963	DU101	DU5824	Sept 62	Aug 63
1964	DU5825	DU13374	Aug 63	Aug 64
1965	DU13375	DU24874	Aug 64	June 65
1966	DU24875	DU44393	Aug 65	July 66
1967	DU44394	DU66245	Sept 66	July 67
1968	DU66246	DU85903	Aug 67	June 68
1969	DU85904	DU90282	July 68	Aug 68
– then (1969)	JC00101	HC24346	Aug 68	July 69
1970	JD24849	ND60540	Aug 69	Oct 70
1971	NE01436	HE30869	Oct 70	July 71
1972	HG30870	not known	Jul 71	May 72
1973 (650)	JH15366	GH36466	Aug 72	June 72

From August 1969 Triumph (and BSA) revised their numbering system to use a two-letter prefix to designate the month and model year of manufacture:

Prefix	Month manufactured	Model year
A	January	1979
B	February	1980
C	March	1969
D	April	1970
E	May	1971
G	June	1972
H	July	1973
J	August	1974
K	September	1975
N	October	1976
P	November	1977
X	December	1978

So a 1970 model year Bonneville manufactured in September 1969 would have a prefix 'KD', while a 1970 model year US market Bonneville manufactured in March 1970 would have the prefix 'CD'.

The system was modified for the model years from 1981, with the addition of new two letter date codes: DA for 1981, EA for 1982 and 1983. So an August 1980 bike has the prefix KDA, while the last bikes, produced in January 1983, were prefixed AEA.

Triumph TR7RV Engine and Frame Numbers				
Model year	*TR7 start no.*	*TR7 finish no.*	*TR7 start date*	*TR7 finish date*
1973	KH17122	GH35466	09/72	16/06/73
1974	JJ58039	JJ58064	30/08/73	31/08/73
1975	GK62244	GK62248	26/06/75	26/06/75
1976	DN70186	EN71867	13/04/76?	26/05/76
1977	HP74444	HP84475	14/07/76	13/07/77
1978	PX02117	HX10584	18/11/77	11/07/78

Triumph T140V Bonneville Engine and Frame Numbers				
Model year	*T140 start no.*	*T140 finish no.*	*T140 start date*	*T140 finish date*
1973	JH15435	GH36466?	Aug 72	June 73
1974	GJ55101	NJ60061	June 73	Oct 74
1975	DK61000	GK62248	April 74	June 75
1976	HN62501	GN72283	July 75	June 76
1977	GP75000	JP84931	June 76	Aug 77
1978	HX00100	HX10747	July 77	July 78

Meriden

The final years of the Meriden Co-op were turbulent but there was a surprisingly large number of new models, over and above the 'basic' Bonneville and Tiger models seen between 1976 and 1978. While the Jubilee Bonneville of 1977 opened Meriden's eyes to the potential of limited edition models, Meriden's first really 'new' model was the 1979 T140D Special, the first of Meriden Triumph's 'factory customs'. As the numbers of bikes the factory could produce slowly reduced, the factory was able to be more flexible in its production-line methods, which allowed it to introduce new models, even if these were based firmly on the basic engine and running gear, with the bespoke engine of the TSS being the honourable exception. This led to the number of different models being produced increasing each year as Meriden chased niche markets: it was rumoured at the time that the factory

would make any combination of features a customer wanted. This final section aims to untangle the somewhat obscure set of Meriden models produced from 1979 to the final production in January 1983.

**1979 Model Year
(July 1978–December 1979)**

T140E Bonneville
Start HA11001 to KA24999, July 1978–
   September 1978
then XB24609 to XB24790, December
   1979 (NB this XB was wrongly marked
   with a 'B' – it should be XA)

T140D Bonneville Special
Start HA11001, July 1978

TR7RV Tiger
Start HA1109 to XA24608, 13 July 1978–14
   December 1979

185

**1980 Model Year
(November 1979–September 1980)**

T140E, T140D
Start PB25001 to KB27500, November
1979–September 1980

T140ES
Start CB29901

TR7RV Tiger
Start PB25193 to JB27513, 26 November
1979–14 August 1980

**1981 Model Year
(August 1980–July 1981)**

**T140E, ES Bonneville, T140E,
ES Executive, T140AV Special Police**
Start KDA28001 to DDA29427

TR7V Tiger, TR7VS Tiger
Start KDA28097 to DDA29398,
22 September 1980–13 April 1981

**1982 Model Year (8 July 1981–
February 1982)**

**T140E, ES Bonneville & Executive,
T140LE Royal**
Start HDA30651 to BDA31693, July
1981–February 1982

**TR7RV, TR7RVS, TR7T Tiger Trail,
TR65 Thunderbird, TR7AV**
Start JDA29428 to BDA31917, 5 May
(August?) 1981–21 February 1982

1983 Model Year (February 1982–)
T140E, ES Bonneville
Start BEA 33001 to AEA34389, February
1982–7 January 1983

T140TSX
Start GEA 33027, June 1982

T140W TSS
Start CEA 33027, March 1982

T140AV Executive
Start GEA 33526, June 1982

**TR7RV, TR7RVS, TR7T, TR7AV,
TR65 Thunderbird 650 (UK and US),
TR6T Tiger Trail 650**
Start BEA33009 to AEA34386, 15 February
1982–7 January 1983

The final Meriden Bonneville was numbered
AEA34389 and the final Meriden Tiger was
numbered AEA34386. Both were produced
on 7 January 1983, after which no more complete machines were produced at Meriden. The
factory and its contents were auctioned off in
December 1983.

The Harris Bonneville was launched on 25
June 1985, starting with engine and frame number 00003, and the final model was produced
on 9 March 1988 with engine frame number
001258.

Bibliography

Bacon, Roy, *Triumph Twins and Triples* (Osprey Publishing Ltd, 1981, rev. 1986); comprehensive history of the post-war models, including lists of engine and frame numbers and general specifications

Brooke, Lindsay, *Triumph Racing Motorcycles in America* (Motorbooks International, 1992); comprehensive coverage of Triumph's competition successes in the USA

Brooke, Lindsay, and Gaylin, David, *Triumph Motorcycles in America* (Motorbooks International, 1993); well-researched and readable history of the Triumph marque in the USA

Clew, Jeff, *Turner's Triumphs: Edward Turner and his Triumph Motorcycles* (Veloce Publishing Ltd, 2000)

Cycle World on Triumph, 1962–1967 (Brooklands Books, 1987)

Cycle World on Triumph, 1967–1972 (Brooklands Books, 1988); collections of road tests, including B-series twins, reprinted from the US magazine *Cycle World*

Gaylin, David, *Triumph Motorcycle Restoration Guide: Bonneville and TR6, 1956–1983* (Motorbooks International, 1997); excellent and detailed history of the US Bonneville and TR6 models, focusing on the specification of each model year

Hopwood, Bert, *Whatever Happened to the British Motorcycle Industry* (Haynes, 1981, rev. 1998); definitive account of the decline and fall of the industry, told by one of its most influential engineers

Nelson, J. R., *Bonnie: The Development History of the Triumph Bonneville* (Haynes Publishing, 1979, rev. 1994); year-by-year development of the T120 Bonneville, written by an ex-Meriden man

Shenton, Stan, *Triumph Tuning* (Lodgemark Press, 1976); detailed descriptions of tuning techniques applied to 500cc, 650cc and 750cc Triumphs by the Boyer racing team of the 1970s, with loads of information on how to make 650cc Triumph twins go faster and hold together

Triumph Bonneville Gold Portfolio, 1959–1983 (Brooklands Books, 1996); collection of road tests of Triumph Bonnevilles, both pre-unit and unit types, taken from UK and US magazines and covering both contemporary and modern 'Classic' titles

Wilson, Steve, *British Motor Cycles since 1950*, v: *Triumph: The Company* (Patrick Stephens Ltd, 1991); vi: *Triumph Motor Cycles since 1950* (Patrick Stephens Ltd, 1983, rev. 1997 as *Triumph Motor Cycles from 1950 to 1988*)

Woolridge, Harry, *The Triumph Speed Twin & Thunderbird Bible* (Veloce Publishing Ltd, 2004); full specifications of the 6T Thunderbirds, loads of detail and good illustrations

Woolridge, Harry, *The Triumph Trophy Bible* (Veloce Publishing Ltd, 2007); model by model coverage of the 'B' Series Trophy and Tiger models, written by an ex-Meriden man with extensive first-hand knowledge of the Triumph marque

Recommended Suppliers

All of the following suppliers provided me with spares and advice during the rebuild, and I can thoroughly recommend them, both in terms of the quality of goods supplied and in the service provided. All the suppliers named are UK-based. Telephone numbers are for UK use; international callers should replace the first '0' with '44'.

Central Wheel Components Ltd
Wheel House, 8 & 9 Station Road, Coleshill, Birmingham B46 1HT
Tel: 01675 462264
Fax: 01675 466412
www.central-wheel.co.uk
Email: info@central-wheel.co.uk

Suppliers of rims and spokes. A supplier I have used for all my restorations, and have always received prompt and knowledgeable service. Rims and spokes have always been of good quality, with a range of options such as 'ordinary' and 'better' quality chrome rims, alloy rims and stainless steel rims. They also supply tyres and will build wheels.

Rockerbox
31 The Street, Wrecclesham, Farnham, Surrey GU10 4QS
Tel: 01252 722973

Support your local motorcycle shop! Triumph spares and mechanical work. Get advice from Darrell, spannering by Arthur, tea by request.

A traditional motorcycle shop, specializing in Triumph parts and complete bikes, but not averse to the odd BSA, Velocette or other British iron.

Hart Motorcycle Services
Redfields Stables, Redfields Lane, Church Crookham, Hants GU52 0RB

Another local bike shop I use. While not stocking specific Triumph spares, they do carry oil and general spares such as batteries, carburettor fittings, cable nipples, tyres and inner tubes. They also do number plates, mechanical work and MoT tests.

Tri-Cor
The Old Hopkiln, Whitwick Manor, Lower Eggleton, Ledbury, Herefordshire HR8 2UE
Tel/Fax: 01432 820752
www.tri-corengland.com
Email: sales@tri-corengland.com

I have used Tri-Cor for many years now (they used to be called Rare Spares) and they have consistently provided excellent service and quality goods. Orders have always been despatched promptly and contained what I had ordered. Tri-Cor also run Sparx, who manufacture various electrical components, including alternators and stators, rectifiers and regulator 'black boxes' (including an excellent 1960s zener diode heat sink lookalike), Lucas-style switchgear and electronic ignition kits.

Vehicle Wiring Products

9 Buxton Court, Manners Industrial Estate,
Ilkeston, Derbyshire DE7 8EF
Tel: 0115 9305454
Fax: 0115 9440101
Email: sales@vehicleproducts.co.uk

Another firm I have used for all my restorations and have received consistently good service. Suppliers of everything you need to rewire a bike, such as bullet connectors, spade terminals and correctly colour-coded wire. They also supply reproduction switches, lights, indicators and electrical fixtures, and some other motorcycle-related items such as control levers.

eBay

A wonderful source of both spares and literature relating to classic bikes – and indeed classic bikes as well. It's an autojumble online. Go to *www.ebay.co.uk* (in the UK) and search for the parts you need, but always remember – buyer beware.

JR Technical Publications

Distributed by Andover Norton International Ltd
3 Old Farm Buildings, Standen Manor Estate,
Hungerford, Berkshire RG17 0RB
Tel: 01488 686816
Fax: 01488 686826
www.andover-norton.co.uk
Email: office@andover-norton.co.uk

Purveyors of original and reproduction Triumph literature. Licensed by the modern Triumph Motorcycles to supply official Triumph literature including parts lists, workshop manuals and handbooks for most Meriden Triumph models … and their reproductions look just as they were in the 1960s and 1970s.

Index